BIZARRE AND ECCENTRIC

Weird People and Extraordinary Lives

LONGMEADOW
P R E S S

This 1992 edition published by Longmeadow Press, 201 High Ridge Road, Stamford, CT 06904.

Cover design by Cooper Wilson

Thanks to the Hulton Picture Company and
Mary Evans Picture Library for sourcing pictures.

Library of Congress Cataloging-in-Publication Data is available upon request

ISBN 0-681-416482

Printed in Czechoslovakia

0 9 8 7 6 5 4 3 2 1

BIZARRE
AND
ECCENTRIC

PALACE INTRUDER
A Royal Audience

Despite security precautions at Buckingham Palace, the Queen of England was disturbed by an intruder as she lay in bed. How did a painter and decorator called Michael Fagan come to be chatting to his monarch as she desperately tried to summon assistance?

Buckingham Palace stands as more than a royal home in London - it is the essence of the monarchy, a symbol that draws hundreds of thousands of visitors a year.

Its imposing gates, and the high wrought-iron railings and barbed wire running along the perimeter walls of the garden are the visible guardians. Unseen are pressure pads, infra-red beams, attack dogs and police and military guards.

Yet every line of defence failed when an unhinged decorator called Michael Fagan decided he would visit his Queen in her bedroom. His break-in ranks as one of the most astonishing stories in the history of the British monarchy.

THE WRONG SIDE OF THE TRACKS

Michael Fagan was born at Paddington General Hospital on 8 August 1950 and was named after his building contractor father. His mother, Ivy, looked after their home on a run-down housing estate built after the war.

At first he seemed a bright boy, but that early promise waned at the tough Sir Philip Magnus secondary school near King's Cross, where he played truant and left at fifteen with no qualifications. Fagan drifted into a succession of handyman and decorating jobs.

In 1972 he married a Welsh girl called Christine, who already had two children by different fathers.

Over the next few years Fagan fathered four more children. Social workers' reports hinted at drug use by Fagan. But while his somewhat quirky lifestyle aroused their concern over his children's safety, there was never any evidence that he was abusive towards them.

Fagan and his bride existed on unemployment and supplementary benefits and child allowances. They moved twelve times in ten years.

The marriage began breaking up about two years before his palace 'visit'. There were angry scenes between him and Christine, which sometimes ended with her leaving the flat with the children. Ivy would console Michael and clean up the flat, which degenerated into squalor whenever he was left to his own devices.

In 1980 the Fagans' marriage started breaking up and Christine walked out on several occasions

On 26 June 1982, thirteen days before he broke into the Palace, he traced his wife to a sordid squat in Islington, North London. After angry scenes he was charged with assaulting his stepson.

But while he languished on remand in Brixton Prison he was visited by Christine and they made up.

*Opposite: **Michael Fagan, a no-hoper in trouble with the law, made his way one morning to the bed chamber of Her Majesty Queen Elizabeth II. He turned the knob and stepped inside...***

*Drop in opposite: **Michael Fagan on his way to court.***

*Below: **The grounds of Buckingham Palace are ringed by high walls and railings, trigger alarms, infra-red beams, attack dogs, police and military guards. Michael Fagan evaded them all.***

But nobody knew that three weeks before the Islington showdown Fagan had been on a secret mission - an undiscovered break-in at Buckingham Palace! On 7 June security in London was allegedly tighter than a thumbscrew for a visit by President Reagan, yet he had scaled the fence undetected.

THE UNINVITED GUEST

Michael Fagan's second, more famous climb occurred in the early hours of Friday 9 July. As he hauled himself over the iron railings, he was seen by an off-duty policeman. The officer alerted his superiors, who immediately instigated a search - but without success.

Fagan first gained entry to the Palace itself through an open window on the ground floor, but the inner doors of the room he entered were locked so he climbed out again. Little did he know that the room housed the Royal Stamp Collection worth £14 million!

After shinning up a drainpipe and walking along a narrow ledge, he peeled back some wire netting to squeeze through a window into the office of the Master of the Household. The window had been opened only minutes earlier by a housemaid. Through this stroke of luck he had penetrated the heart of the Palace.

In his climb Fagan had triggered one of the infra-red alarms, but a policeman

in the Palace switched it off, thinking it was a malfunction.

For the next fifteen minutes Fagan wandered unchallenged through the corridors and rooms of Buckingham Palace. He was seen by a maid who didn't think his behaviour was suspicious, so she did not report him.

Later he told police that he found his way to the private apartments by 'following the pictures' by Rembrandt, Turner and others which cover the Palace walls. Before he entered the Queen's bedroom he went into an ante-room and smashed a glass ashtray, cutting his hand.

At 7.15am, clutching a jagged piece of glass from the broken ashtray, he gingerly turned the knob on the Queen's door and let himself in.

The Queen was awoken as Fagan stepped across the floor to the heavy curtains and thrust them aside, letting the sun flood into the room.

What thoughts raced through Her Majesty's mind as she saw the sock-clad prowler, glass in his bloodied hand, can only be guessed at. She has never spoken publicly about the incident.

But it is a measure of her character that she remained level-headed and calm when many people would have screamed. The one thing she could not afford to do with the staring-eyed stranger was to lose her head or antagonize him.

What thoughts raced through Her Majesty's mind as she looked up from her bed and saw the prowler?

The Queen, well rehearsed in emergency procedures by the Royal Protection Squad officers who guard her, pressed the night bell connected to the police sentry on duty in the corridor outside. But at 6am the police sergeant - in accordance with Scotland Yard instructions - had left for the night.

The footman who would normally have been outside was away exercizing the Queen's corgis, while a maid was vacuuming in another room.

Fagan sat at the edge of her bed in filthy jeans and a tattered T-shirt. What the Queen didn't know then was the plan that had gelled in Fagan's disturbed mind

Below: Police guarding the Queen were slammed for their mistakes. Security at the Palace has since been improved.

after he had smashed the ashtray. 'He intended to commit suicide on the Queen's bed,' said the police report.

The Queen pretended she wanted a cigarette - a habit she abhorred - and asked Fagan if he would like one. He replied that he would, and she then rang through to the Palace switchboard operator with a request that a policeman should bring her some.

Fagan later told his lawyer, Maurice Nadeem: 'We talked about our children. She told me she has a son called Charles who had a baby with Princess Diana. She said I must be very proud of my four children, that it would not be right for me to kill myself and leave them without a father. She was so kind to think of me in a situation like that.'

The first call went unanswered for six minutes. Her Majesty was furious. Everyone in the Palace knew that she did not smoke - so why on earth should she be ordering cigarettes from the privacy of her bedroom? She apologised to Fagan and phoned again, asking why her previous call had been ignored.

Chambermaid Elizabeth Andrews then entered the Queen's bedroom after cleaning in the other room, and is said to have greeted the Queen with the immortal words: 'Bloody 'ell ma'am! What's he doing in here?'

The Queen politely told her maid that Mr Fagan wanted a cigarette, and together they led him into a pantry where a footman came and chatted to him.

'Bloody 'ell, ma'am!' cried the chambermaid. 'What's he doing here?'

Within another two minutes first one, then another, police officer arrived and Fagan was led away. The nightmare had lasted less than a quarter of an hour.

AFTER THE EVENT

That there had been an appalling series of blunders was plain for all to see. A harshly worded internal Scotland Yard report laid the blame squarely at the door of the police.

Home Secretary William Whitelaw concurred, adding: 'It was an appalling

Top: *The Queen demonstrated her usual composure when the intruder walked across her bedroom to the curtains*

Above: *Fagan, who arrived wild-eyed at the Queen's bedside...clutching a jagged piece of glass from a broken ashtray.*

lapse of security. The Queen handled the intrusion with great composure.'

Assistant Police Commissioner John Dellow said: 'The cause of the breakdown of security was a failure by police to respond efficiently. If police officers had been alert Fagan would have been apprehended well before he got close to the private apartments.'

The unbalanced Fagan understandably was not prosecuted for the intrusion into the Queen's inner sanctum, and he was acquitted of stealing wine during the first trespass. However he still faced prior charges of assault and theft of a car, for which he served time in a mental institution until 1983.

His only public comment on his 'royal audience' was through a statement, read out by his lawyer, in which he dismissed speculation that the monarch's life was threatened. He never took up Fleet Street newspapers' offers to pay him thousands of pounds to hear his tale of a morning with the Queen.

JUNGLE SOLDIERS
The War that Went On

World War II ended in 1945, a fact that some Japanese soldiers never discovered. Fanatically loyal to their Emperor, they hid in the jungle for decades rather than risk the disgrace of capture

They were the descendants of the Knights of Bushido - Samurai warriors who excelled in war and knew no other life. Their creed was one of total obedience to their Emperor, their earthly mission none other than duty and death. Capture to them was the ultimate disgrace before Emperor and God, the humiliation that would brand them forever in the eyes of those whom they held in esteem - friends, family, officers, priests.

Such was the mentality of the average Japanese soldier in World War II - soldiers who fought to the death in their hundreds of thousands, or fell upon their own swords, rather than fly the white flag of surrender to the Allied forces.

For the Americans in particular, whose Marine Corps, Navy and Air Force crews

Above: *US soldiers wade ashore from a landing craft onto a Japanese-held Pacific island.*

Opposite: *On 9 August, 1945 the United States dropped the world's second-only atomic device on the Japanese city of Nagasaki.*

Below: *The Japanese city of Osaka was devastated by American air raids as World War II drew to a close.*

performed stupendous feats clearing the Pacific islands of the invaders, the names of places like Iwo Jima, Tarawa and Guadalcanal are written in blood on their memories. The Japanese turned these placid atolls into impregnable redoubts where every inch of sand was contested.

Thank God, said those who had lived through it, that it was all over in August 1945 when the Japanese Emperor Hirohito told his people to 'endure the unendurable' and lay down their arms in surrender.

But there were many soldiers who did not hear - and therefore could not heed - the call to surrender. For years afterwards they lived in the jungles and bush of the South Pacific and Indonesia, their Imperial Army uniforms reduced to rags on their backs, existing only to carry on the struggle against the Allies.

These men knew nothing of atom bombs which blasted apart their cities, nor the fire raids on Tokyo which levelled the metropolis. In their tropical lairs they did not know of a signed surrender on the USS *Missouri* in Tokyo Bay, nor of the occupation of their homeland. They slept at dusk and rose every day at dawn in the belief that the war was still going on.

Rumours of this lost legion of soldiers echoed down the years. Trappers in remote Philippine villages heard the tales of the 'devil men' living like jungle beasts in dens. In Indonesia they talked

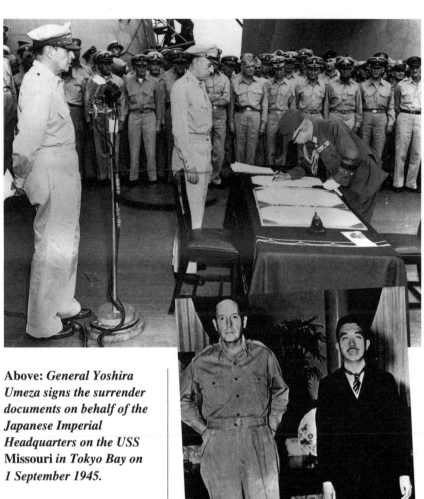

Above: *General Yoshira Umeza signs the surrender documents on behalf of the Japanese Imperial Headquarters on the USS Missouri in Tokyo Bay on 1 September 1945.*

Right: *The Allied Supremo General Douglas MacArthur towers beside Japan's Emperor Hirohito. MacArthur remained effective ruler of Japan until 1950.*

A WORLD OF CONCEALMENT

It was on 14 October, 1944 that time froze for Masashi, Private 1st Class in the Army of His Imperial Highness the Emperor of Japan. He bent down to tie his bootlaces on a military road on the island as his comrades marched ahead...straight into an ambush sprung by Australian troops. As the sound of gunfire crackled through the undergrowth Masashi made a dive for the foliage with his comrade, Corporal Iroki Minakawa.

Over and over they rolled as the gunfire and sound of grenades echoed through the undergrowth. It was the start of their incredible sixteen-year game of hide-and-seek with the outside world.

For the first two months the private and the corporal existed on emergency rations and grubs that they scavenged from the forest floor. They drank rainwater collected in banana leaves, chewed the roots of edible plants for fibre, and occasionally dined on snakes caught in traps which they fashioned with wire from their backpacks and twigs.

During this early stage in their jungle exile they were hunted by Allied soldiers and later by native Chamorra aborigines with their wild dogs. At night they fashioned primitive hides and developed a new language - tongue clicks and hand signs which they considered the only safe form of communication.

They established a series of animal-like hides dug into the forest floor and covered with foliage. They lined the floor with dried grass and planted sharpened stakes in pits nearby to trap food.

To avoid being overheard by Allied troops they developed a language of tongue clicks and silent gestures

---

For an astonishing eight years they lived a nomadic existence.

Masashi later said: *During this harsh period we would often stumble across many other groups of Japanese soldiers who, like ourselves, had never given up the struggle. We felt sure that our generals had only made a tactical withdrawal and would one day come back with reinforcements.*

of the 'yellow ones' still roaming the dense undergrowth. The West, with its own problems of reconstruction, ignored these reports and they had adopted the aura of folk legends.

In 1961, however, sixteen years after the fall of Japan, a soldier named Ito Masashi emerged from the tropical jungles of Guam to surrender. Like a man emerging from some cocooned sleep, Masashi could not believe that the world he believed in so forcefully in 1945 no longer existed.

He had spent his years in hiding sure in the knowledge that his Emperor still needed him and that it was only a matter of time before his comrades came back for him.

We sometimes made fires but there was always the danger of the natives spotting them. The Japanese soldiers either died of starvation or disease, or were attacked and killed by the natives. I knew I had to stay alive because it was my duty to do so. It was only thanks to the good fortune of finding an American airbase's rubbish dump that we survived. The rubbish dump became a life-giving source for the fugitive soldiers. The extravagant GIs threw away an endless variety of food. They also found tin cans which they made into eating and cooking pans. Sewing needles were made from bedsprings, while primitive sheets were cobbled together from tents.

Every year the rainy season was their worst enemy, when for two months they would sit sullenly in their hides as the rains pelted down and they existed on berries and frogs which they drowned in pails of water. The tension between the two of them was almost unbearable during these times, said Masashi.

One day during the monsoon there was a terrible row between the men, forcing Minakawa to leave. Masashi recalled: *After he had gone I had an urge to scream at the top of my voice. I knew I could not survive without human company. For days I crawled through the dense jungle clicking my tongue until I heard his clicking signal. We embraced and vowed never to part again.*

The soldiers lacked salt in their diet so at night they sneaked down to the coast to boil sea water and eat the salt crystals.

MISTRUST AND DISBELIEF

After ten years they found leaflets on the island. They contained a message from a Japanese general whom neither of them had ever heard of, urging them to surrender. Masashi said: 'I knew that it was a ploy put out by the Americans to trap us. I said to Minakawa: "What kind of fools do they take us for?" '

The men's incredible devotion to a code of duty alien to many Westerners is illustrated by another incident Masashi recalls: *Once Minakawa and I thought about escaping by sea. We walked miles along the coastline looking for a boat in vain. What we did find was one of the*

two American barracks ablaze with lights. We crept near enough to see men and women dancing together and to hear the sound of a jazz tune. That was the first time that we had set our eyes on women in years and I was filled with despair at what I had been missing! Back in my shelter I began to carve the figure of a nude woman from a piece of old tree trunk. We could easily have walked over to the American camp and surrendered - I did not think then that they would harm us - but it was not in my spirit. I was bound to the Emperor and he would have been disappointed in us.

I still did not think the war was over but that the Emperor had merely pulled the troops out to fight elsewhere.

Masashi was shown a picture of his memorial in Japan, which stated that he had been killed in action

---

One morning, after sixteen years in hiding, Masashi's comrade put on his home-made wooden sandals and went off to steal a chicken. But twenty-four hours later he had not returned. Masashi was gripped by panic. 'I knew I could not survive without him,' he said. *I blundered through the jungle to search for him. I reached a military road, where I found Minakawa's rucksack and his sandals. I felt certain then that he had been captured by the Americans.*

Above: *Islanders on Guam captured soldiers Masashi and Minakawa. Both thought the war was still on 16 years after it had ended!*

Below: *Straggler Hiroo Onoda held out for 29 years in the jungle of Lubang island in the Philippines.*

Suddenly a helicopter swooped overhead and I scuttled back into the jungle, resolving to die fighting them. I climbed up a mountain and there were four Americans waiting for me. One of the 'Americans' was Minakawa with a freshly shaved face! He told me that natives had caught him stealing and had turned him over to the Americans. He said the war was over but it took me months in captivity before I would believe it. I was shown a picture of my memorial in Japan, saying I had been killed in action.

Reality was hard to take. All my youth wasted on a lost venture. I had so much living to catch up on. The first night I had a warm bath and a sleep between clean sheets . It was indescribably good.

FURTHER SURVIVORS FROM THE FORESTS

The emergence of Masashi was topped twelve years later, in 1972, by that of Shoichi Yokoi, a sergeant in the Imperial Army. He too had been on Guam.

When the Americans stormed the island he fled from his 77th Marine and Infantry Regiment and found a cave in the foothills of the mountains. He too found the leaflets littering the jungle floor urging Japanese soldiers to surrender in accordance with their

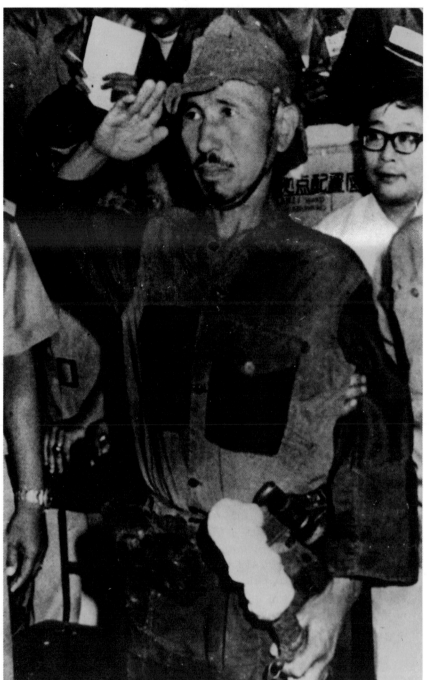

Above: *A gaunt-looking Lieutenant Onoda finally acknowledges that the war is over. He only surrendered when his former superior officer ordered him to do so.*

Left: *Onoda photographed when he was 23. He survived in the jungle by raiding villages for food and provisions - to the great terror of the villagers.*

Emperor's decree; and he, too, refused to believe them.

A hermit without the company of a fellow soldier, he hunted frogs and rats to survive. He wove clothes from tree-bark when his uniform rotted off his back, and shaved by scraping his face with sharpened flints.

He said: *It was so lonely for so many nights. I went to shout once at a snake that had crawled into the entrance of the cave and just a squeak came out. My vocal cords were so unused to being used that they had ceased to function. Every day after that I sang a little song or said a little prayer to keep them functioning.*

He was eventually caught by hunters in January 1972 when, aged fifty-eight, he was told that his exile had been futile. He broke down and wept. He knew nothing of atomic bombs, the surrender or the devastation of his homeland. When he was taken to hospital for a check-up - where he was pronounced A-1 fit - he was told he would fly back to Japan aboard a jet which would take three hours. 'What's a jet?' he asked.

When told he would be returned to Japan in a jet, Yokoi asked: 'What's a jet?'

The government in Tokyo was forced by public opinion to launch a drive to bring old soldiers out of their jungle lairs. So they embarked on Operation Cherry Blossom, dropping tons of leaflets on the Philippine islands and other remote atolls that had once been occupied by the Japanese Army. But it failed to flush out a single soldier – they still regarded the leaflets as propaganda by the troops.

THE REMNANTS OF THE IMPERIAL ARMY

Then in 1974 Lieutenant Hiroo Onoda, aged fifty-two, walked out of a Philippine jungle on remote Lubang island and into the arms of the local authorities.

It took his former commanding officer to come and finally talk him into believing the war was over. He asked to be allowed to retain his sacred ceremonial samurai sword, which he had buried on the island in 1945.

Six months before his capture Onoda and a comrade called Kinshicki Kozuka, had ambushed a Philippine Army patrol, mistaking them for Americans. His friend died in the ambush, and efforts to track down Onoda intensified.

Onoda was so bewildered by returning to the twentieth century that he spent four months undergoing intensive psychological counselling. He told doctors: 'I know that there are many of my comrades still out there, I know where they hide and I know their calling signs. But they will never come out for me because they will think that I have

gone soft and have surrendered. They will unfortunately die in those hills.'

Onoda said the only bright spot for him was an abundance of back pay and accumulated pension rights, which he pledged to spend on saki and sushi. There was an emotional meeting between him and his elderly parents back in Japan at which his father said: 'I am so proud of you. You did the right thing because your heart said to do it.'

A year later Lee Kuang-Huei, a native of Taiwan who had signed up for military service with Japan during World War II, was found in a home made hut, on an Indonesian island, sharpening the bamboo spears he used for fishing at night. He flung himself at the feet of the native intruders, who were accompanied by a local police official, and asked to be executed as he had now offended the Emperor by being captured.

If there are any soldiers left now they will be old men, weakening under the strain of such a harsh existence. But deprived of fatty foods, junk food, alcohol and additives, most of the survivors were amazingly fit when their war finally ended.

Nevertheless, at Japanese Shinto and Buddhist shrines around the country, it is a tradition to burn incense and light candles in remembrance of the 'lost ones', the boys who never came back and who never stopped fighting.

Below: *Fourteen years after the war a group of Japanese scoured the Philippine islands of Rabual and Lubang in the search for the two soldiers still hiding in the jungles.*

OCEAN DEATH TRAP
The Bermuda Triangle

Over a hundred aircraft and ships, their crew and passengers, have vanished for no reason in an area off the Florida coast - the infamous Bermuda Triangle. What strange and sinister force is at work here?

On the afternoon of 5 December 1945, the fourteen crewmen of Flight 19 climbed aboard their five US Navy Avenger bombers. It was 2pm and sunny when the aircraft's single engines roared into life and, in perfect flying weather, the planes soared skywards from their base at Fort Lauderdale, Florida, to begin a routine training mission over the Atlantic.

The only thing out of the ordinary was that one of the crew, for no apparent reason, asked and was permitted to be taken off the mission.

The squadron, led by Lieutenant Charles Taylor, thought little of the matter, made simple adjustments for a light north-east wind, then pointed their snub-nosed planes east towards the Bahamas.

The planes, each with enough fuel to cover 1000 miles (a healthy margin for any error), were to fly 160 miles due east, turn to the north for 40 miles, then head south-west back to their base. During their journey they were to make practice bombing runs at target wrecks on a bank called Chicken Shoals.

The five planes and their fourteen crew were never seen again.

Not, that is, until 16 May, 1991, when American treasure hunters seeking a Spanish galleon made an astonishing find. The explorers, diving from the San Francisco research vessel the *Deep See*

Opposite: *The fuselage of an Avenger aircraft resting on the sea bed. The plane is probably one of five that disappeared mysteriously off the Florida coast in December 1945.*

Below: *This Avenger torpedo bomber, photographed in June 1945, was the lead plane in the so-called Lost Squadron. These crewmen were the lucky ones, however - their places had been taken by others when the planes vanished.*

reported that they had located what may well have been the lost squadron which had disappeared forty-five years earlier. The sophisticated craft found the five planes in 750ft of water within two miles of one another, only ten miles off the Florida coast.

The discovery seemed to have put paid to one of the most enduring of the globe's mysteries - that of the notorious Bermuda Triangle. But had it?

EERIE LIGHTS AND STRANGE MALFUNCTIONS

More than a thousand other airmen, sailors and passengers have disappeared over the years, in more than a hundred lost aircraft and ships. Among seamen, the Bermuda Triangle is also known as the Triangle of Death, the Hoodoo Sea and the Graveyard of the Atlantic.

For centuries voyagers have been baffled by its mysterious calms and sudden storms, even from the time that Christopher Columbus entered this stretch of ocean and noted in his log that the crew had sighted peculiar glowing streaks of 'white water'. These eerie patches of lights and foam are still regularly sighted today.

Sometimes they are so bright that they have been detected from outer space. The Apollo 12 astronauts reported that this luminosity was the last light visible to them as they left the Earth.

Mysterious calms, waterspouts and unheralded storms have been chronicled by those bold enough to traverse the danger zone. Apparent instrument malfunction, spinning compass needles and inexplicable, localized deterioration of flying weather bedevil aviators. Often the only warning of these strange environmental changes is a weird yellow haze blanketing the horizon.

Even the fish get confused by the quirky magnetics of the region, and have been observed swimming upside down

---

The US Navy, which lost their five planes in 1945, still does not recognize the Bermuda Triangle as a danger zone, and the US Coast Guard insist that most of the tragedies and disappearances can be explained by the region's unique environmental features.

These include the swiftly flowing Gulf Stream current, the uncharted underwater canyons of that part of the Atlantic, and the terrifyingly violent storms that erupt there without warning.

The Bermuda Triangle is also known to pose a very real, physical threat to the unwary navigator on the sea or in the air. For it is one of the only two places on Earth where the compass needle points to the true, not the magnetic, north.

A navigator can be heading in the wrong direction while being absolutely certain that he is on the correct route. Perhaps this is why even the fish in the area can become confused; divers have reported erratic activity, with fish sometimes swimming upside down.

NO REASONABLE EXPLANATION

These are the logical explanations for the absolutely inexplicable. As officials of the US National Oceanic and Atmospheric Administration state in a report: 'Despite efforts by the US Air Force, Navy and Coast Guard no reasonable explanation to date has been found for the vanishments.'

And Richard Winer, who wrote *The Devil's Triangle*, a book that has sold 2 million copies, says: 'There are mysterious and strange things that are going on out there. I believe that not all the answers lie in human error, mechanical malfunctions, freak weather and magnetic anomalies.'

From the measured arguments of author Winer to those of John Wallace Spencer, an expert on UFOs, who wrote *Limbo of the Lost*, a book that has also sold 2 million copies. His explanations tend to be more fanciful.

Spencer argues that beings from outer space have established a colony under the sea. There, he claims, the missing ships, planes and their crews are kept for scientific research by these aliens of vastly higher intelligence. He says: 'Sure it sounds weird but it's the only explanation that covers all the facts.' Theories involving aliens from outer

space crop up time and time again in the sagas woven around the losses attributed to the Bermuda Triangle. Many claim that flying saucers spirited the ships and aircraft away, rather than sank them.

Such stories may be traced back to a naval board of inquiry called in to examine the mystery of the 1945 Lost Patrol. During the hearing one of the board reflected, 'They vanished as completely as if they had flown to Mars.'

Is this enigmatic stretch of ocean the site of the lost continent of Atlantis?

Another report given in evidence at the time was by a radio ham who claimed he had picked up the frightened voice of a pilot saying: 'Don't come after me - they look like they are from outer space.'

This intrigued Charles Berlitz, grandson of the founder of the Berlitz language schools, and a Yale graduate with a fascination for the legendary lost 'continent' of Atlantis.

Berlitz's theory was that the city that

formed the core of Atlantis was powered by a giant solar crystal which now lies beneath the ocean floor. This crystal, said Berlitz, now sends false messages to the instruments of craft above - and sometimes sucks them to the depths.

Berlitz wrote the bestselling sixties book *The Bermuda Triangle*, itemizing over 140 known disappearances.

THE DOOMED SHIPS

But the actual label 'Bermuda Triangle' was first coined by Vincent Gaddis, the American author of a book on sea mysteries. He wrote: 'Draw a line from Florida to Bermuda, another from Bermuda to Puerto Rico, and a third line back to Florida through the Bahamas. Within this roughly triangular area most of the vanishments have occurred'.

Since his statement, reporters have 'stretched' the Bermuda Triangle into many contorted shapes to help explain - or dramatize - other historical disappearances. But this does not detract from the very many genuine mysteries that have sprung up within that precise,

Above: *Treasure hunters from the San Francisco-based* **Deep See** *discovered what were probably the remains of the Lost Sqadron in May 1991 - 46 years after the planes disappeared off Florida. Here, Captain Keith Calloway and submersible robot designer Graham Hawkes hold up a map showing the spot where they discovered the wrecks.*

enigmatic and very dangerous 'Triangle'.

Take, for instance, the case of the British frigate *Atlanta,* which in January 1880 set sail from Bermuda for England with a crew of 290, most of them young training cadets. The ship vanished without trace, despite one of the most thorough searches of all time.

Six vessels of the Channel Fleet patrolled in line abreast, each only a mile apart, over the area where the *Atlanta* had disappeared. The search went on for four months, but not a single item of wreckage was found.

A year later came the first of at least a dozen instances of 'ghost' ships found floating crewless within the Bermuda Triangle. In 1881 the cargo ship *Ellen Austin* came upon a schooner with its sails billowing in the wind. Aboard was a full cargo of mahogany - but no sign of human life.

The captain of the *Ellen Austin* could not believe his luck. He decided the derelict ship would be his prize and put men on board her.

Suddenly a fierce squall caused the two ships to lose sight of one another. It was two days before the *Ellen Austin* saw its captured ship again - strangely, drifting once more. The crew who had been ordered aboard it were gone.

But the story does not end there. The greedy captain was determined to secure the schooner at all costs. After using all his powers of persuasion to get yet another crew on board, a further storm arose...and the mysterious ship plus her new crew was never seen again.

The first mystery that the twentieth century threw up was the disappearance of the supply ship USS *Cyclops* in 1918. On 4 March this state-of-the-art piece of engineering, all 500 ft and 19,500 tons of her, set sail from Barbados for Norfolk, Virginia with a valuable cargo of manganese ore and a crew of 309.

Because World War I was still in progress when the *Cyclops* vanished, it was first thought that the vessel had been the victim of a German mine or submarine. But this theory was later dismissed when access was made available to German war records. Careful study revealed that no mines had been laid nor any submarine positioned in

Above: *The US Navy supply ship* Cyclops *vanished in March 1918, during the last months of World War I. At first, it was assumed that a U-boat or mine had sunk it, but research in German records after the war showed that no U-boats or mines were anywhere in the vicinity.*

those waters at that time.

At the time of her disappearance the weather had been fair, the seas moderate and winds light, ruling out the obvious explanations of storm damage or shifting cargo.

The Royal Navy reported: 'The disappearance of the ship has been one of the most baffling mysteries in the annals of the Navy.'

As the century grew older, more examples were recorded of the jinx afflicting the area yet to be labelled the Bermuda Triangle.

In 1925 the American freighter *Cotopaxi,* bound for Havana from Charleston, simply disappeared. The following year the cargo tramp *Suduffco* never completed its journey from Newark, New Jersey to Puerto Rico.

The Norwegian freighter *Stavanger* vanished off the face of the earth with its

in cargo, size and age. But they had two things in common - none of them gave out any distress calls at all, despite all having radios on board. And there were no severe weather or storm conditions when they disappeared.

What we do know is that extensive searches throughout the waters of the Triangle have never produced any evidence of a cause for these vessels or their crews going missing.

The pattern, however, was broken in the case of the Japanese freighter *Raifuku Maru*. During the winter of 1924 she gave out a chilling message from somewhere between the Bahamas and Cuba.

The last words heard from her were: 'Danger like a dagger now...Come quickly...We cannot escape...' No one has ever discovered what that danger was. Even more mysterious was that a ship steaming towards the *Raifuku Maru* after hearing the distress call found nothing: no wreckage, no bodies. The Triangle had claimed another victim.

FLIGHT TO OBLIVION

Because of heightened military security during World War II less public awareness was created about the so-called Hoodoo Sea. Until 5 December 1945, when the five US Navy Avenger bombers set off on their ill-fated flight.

An hour after take-off, with their mock bombing runs completed, the Fort Lauderdale control tower received an urgent radio message from Lieutenant Charles Taylor. 'Calling tower,' he radioed. 'This is an emergency. We seem to be off course. We cannot see land. Repeat, we cannot see land.'

Tower: 'What is your position?'

Taylor: 'We are not sure of our position. We cannot be sure just where we are. We seem to be lost.'

Tower: 'Assume bearing due west.'

As long as the aircraft were off the Florida coast, this would inevitably have brought the planes back to landfall.

Taylor: 'We don't know which way is west. Everything is wrong...Strange... We cannot be sure of any direction. Even the ocean doesn't look the way it should.'

Although most of his colleagues were

crew of forty-three in 1931. Its last recorded sighting was somewhere south of Cat Island in the Bahamas.

In 1932 the schooner *John and Mary* was found bobbing quietly in calm seas fifty miles south of Bermuda, its sails neatly furled but with not a soul aboard. Another schooner, the *Gloria Colite* from the West Indian island of St Vincent, was found abandoned in 1940.

No distress signals were picked up from any of the vessels, despite having radios on board

---

And in 1944 the Cuban freighter *Rubicon* was similarly found drifting off the Florida coast - its only occupant a dog.

Every one of the vessels mentioned so far was completely different. Each varied still under instruction, Lieutenant Taylor was a highly experienced pilot. It was an unbelievable admission that he did not know his own position and his direction of flight.

About fifteen minutes later, at 3.30pm, a flight instructor at the airbase listened in to the radio and heard, over the static, a conversation between one of the lost pilots and a colleague. The first pilot was asking for compass readings and the second pilot responded with: 'I don't know where we are. We must have got lost after that last turn.'

Increasingly concerned for his seemingly bewildered airmen, the flight instructor desperately attempted to get a message to Lieutenant Taylor. Eventually he succeeded.

Taylor told him: 'I'm sure I'm in the Keys but I don't know how far down.'

We cannot be sure of any direction. Even the ocean doesn't look the way it should

---

By now those commanding the Fort Lauderdale naval station were incredulous. The Florida Keys begin more than a hundred miles to the south - so far off the planes' route as to be unthinkable. If they were heading westwards for 'home' they would find themselves hopelessly lost in the Gulf of Mexico.

The Fort Lauderdale instructor reached Taylor once more and told him to turn to the north.

'We have just passed over a small island,' Taylor reported shortly afterwards. 'No other land in sight.' From that moment onwards, the base was unable to speak to the pilots.

But through the static they were able to pick up snatches of conversation between the airmen. It appeared from the tangle of voices that Taylor had handed over command of the squadron to another senior pilot, Captain Stiver.

At one stage the new leader said: 'We are not sure where we are. We think we must be 225 miles south-east of base. We must have passed over Florida and be in the Gulf of Mexico.'

Later Stiver was heard to say that he was turning 180 degrees in the hope of heading north to hit the Florida coast. No one at base could understand why, in fine weather, the pilots were not using the sun to navigate themselves out of trouble.

The last faint words from the lost squadron were: 'Entering white water. We are completely lost...'

As far as Fort Lauderdale could calculate, the squadron had turned west and begun a flight to oblivion - straight out across the endless wastes of the Atlantic Ocean - while the last of their fuel burned away.

A Martin Mariner flying boat with a crew of thirteen was sent up to hunt for the planes. It radioed back that it had encountered strong winds at 6000ft. Then there was silence.

Coast Guard cutters, destroyers, submarines and Royal Air Force planes, plus a host of private craft, all joined the search. But neither the squadron nor the flying boat was ever seen again...

Until 1991, when the underwater explorers of the research vessel the *Deep See* reported: 'We think we've found the lost squadron.' First underwater cameras and then robots were sent down and confirmed the Fort Lauderdale numbering on the planes. A figure 28 was clearly seen on video. It was Lieutenant Taylor's aircraft.

The fate of Flight 19 was suddenly back in the hands of the living. And some of the mystery that had hung like an enigmatic haze over the Bermuda Triangle had suddenly evaporated.

At least, that is what the experts were saying. Just as they were saying it in 1955 when twelve of them - all Japanese scientists with the most advanced equipment that money could buy - launched an expedition into the Triangle to debunk, once and for all, the legendary curse. They were never heard from again.

Since the disappearance of the ill-fated Flight 19 on 5 December 1945, an astonishing catalogue of mysteries has emanated from the Bermuda Triangle. Here are some of those lost in the graveyard of the Atlantic...

1947: A US Army C54 Superfort disappeared a hundred miles off Bermuda without broadcasting a word to indicate it was in any difficulty.

1948: A British airliner, the *Star Tiger*, a four-engined Tudor-Four, radioed four hundred miles north-east of Bermuda: 'Expect to arrive on schedule.' The thirty-one passengers and crew were never found.

1949: The *Star Ariel*, sister plane of the *Star Tiger*, was flying from London to Santiago in Chile via Bermuda and Jamaica. Radio contact was lost 380 miles south-west of Bermuda. Its last words were: 'All's well.'

1950: The SS *Sandra*, a 350ft freighter, sailed from Savannah, Georgia for Puerto Caballo, Venezuela with 300 tons of insecticide. She passed St Augustine, Florida and then disappeared without trace.

1954: A US Navy Lockheed Super Constellation vanished while flying from Maryland to the Azores.

1955: The yacht *Connemara IV* was found mysteriously abandoned four hundred miles west of Bermuda.

1956: US Navy patrol of Martin seaplanes P5M disappeared with a crew of ten near Bermuda.

1962: US Air Force tanker KB150, flying from Langley Field, Virginia to the Azores, never arrived.

1963: The *Sno-Boy*, a 63ft fishing boat with forty aboard, sailed from Kingston, Jamaica for North-East Cay eighty miles south, but vanished with all hands.

1963: Two new US Air Force KC135 four-engined Stratotankers from Homestead Air Force Base, Florida, heading for a classified refuelling range in the Atlantic, were lost three hundred miles south-west of Bermuda.

1963: AC132 Cargomaster vanished *en route* to the Azores.

1965: AC199 Flying Boxcar with ten aboard vanished in the south-east Bahamas.

1967: The *Revonoc*, an all-weather 46ft racing yacht, disappeared within sight of land.

1967: The owner and passenger of the cabin cruiser *Witchcraft*, disappeared while the vessel was at a harbour buoy just one mile from Miami.

1970: The *Milton Latrides*, a freighter *en route* from New Orleans to Cape Town, vanished.

1973: The *Anita*, a 20,000 ton freighter with a crew of thirty-two, sailing from Newport News to Hamburg, disappeared.

1984: The brig *Marques*, 88ft, foundered during the world-famous Tall Ships Race and was lost with eighteen crew on the northern borders of the Bermuda Triangle.

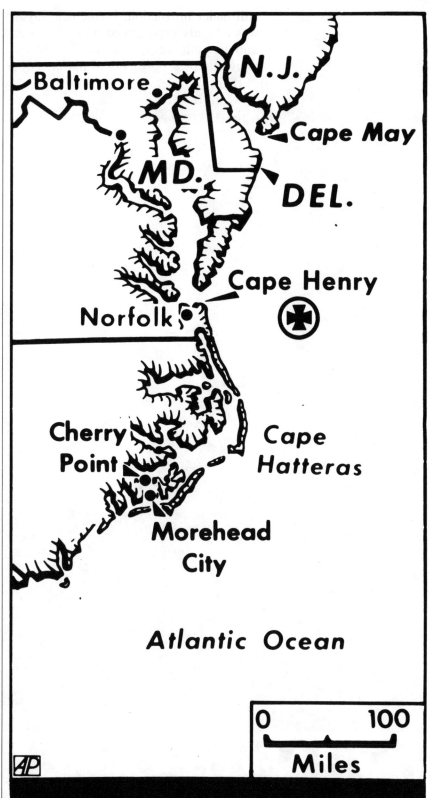

Above: A map shows the spot where the USS Cyclops disappeared during World War I. The ship had been sailing between Barbados in the West Indies and Norfolk, Virginia.

CASPAR HAUSER
Mystery Child

The enigma of Caspar Hauser was a topic of animated discussion throughout the drawing rooms and taverns of nineteenth-century Europe. Was he of royal blood, as some believed, or a child of the devil?

By the early nineteenth century, the Southern German city of Nuremberg was a bustling provincial centre. Its wide cobbled streets were lined with elegant houses, its fine squares graced with ornate churches and fountains. Into this 'Treasure House of Germany' came a shabbily dressed waif, a pauper who may have been a prince...

THE ENIGMA ARRIVES IN NUREMBERG

On a bright May morning in 1812 a cobbler called Georg Weichmann squinted across the square outside his home at the shambling figure which emerged from an alleyway. It was a boy of about sixteen, dressed in a torn topcoat and tattered knee-breeches. He hobbled unsteadily in a pair of ill-fitting boots.

The kindly cobbler instantly took pity on the lad and walked over to where he stood, staring wildly about him as though in a panic. 'Are you lost? Where are your parents?' asked Weichmann.

All the cobbler's questions produced merely strange, unintelligible whispers until, suddenly, the child thrust an envelope into his hand. The address read: 'The Captain of the 4th Squadron, 6th Cavalry Regiment.'

Puzzled, the cobbler led him to the Captain's house nearby. The Captain was not at home, and while they waited his servant offered them food.

Weichmann was amazed when the waif, thin as he was, refused to touch a plate of meat and sausage in front of him, but instead grabbed a dry bread roll and ate it ravenously.

Eventually the Captain arrived and tore open the envelope to find two letters.

The first was dated a few days before. It read: 'I send you a boy who is anxious to serve his country in the Army. He was left on my doorstep as a baby. I have ten children of my own to bring up and can care for him no longer.' The note ended callously: 'If you do not want to keep him, kill him or hang him up a chimney.'

The second letter was dated 1812 and purported to be from the child's natural mother. It said simply: 'Take care of my child. His father was in the 6th Cavalry.'

'If you do not want to keep him,' ran the letter, 'kill him or hang him up a chimney'.

The Captain took one disdainful look at the child and decided to wash his hands of the whole strange affair. Despite the protestations of the kindly cobbler, the boy was promptly marched off to the nearest police station and thrown into a cell. For several days, while his fate was being decided, a jailer watched the child and was struck by what he saw.

'He can sit for hours without moving a limb,' he observed later. 'He sits rigidly without growing at all uncomfortable. Also he prefers darkness to light and can move about in it like a cat.' The jailer gave the child a scrap of paper on which he scratched the words 'Reiter' - the German for cavalryman - and 'Caspar Hauser'. This, police assumed, was the boy's name.

In many of his actions he would appear babylike, often tottering on his feet and falling like a toddler who was only just learning to walk. Yet Caspar seemed to have a bright, alert mind. The patient jailer spent hours every day teaching him to speak and write.

A STRANGE TALE

Within six weeks Caspar could at last relate the story of the first sixteen years of his wretched life, and the jailer summoned the city Burgomaster to hear his sad tale.

Above: *Caspar Hauser arrived with a note in his hand at the city of Nuremberg one morning in May 1812...an enigma was born.*

Opposite: *The young Caspar remembered being kept in a tiny darkened room, slumbering on rags laid across a straw bed. He was fed on bread and water and was possibly drugged.*

Above: Hauser admires a wooden horse watched over by Professor Daumer in this early print. Under caring tuition, this backward boy became a youthful academic.

Caspar could remember being kept locked up all day and all night in a small darkened room about six feet by four. He slept in rags on a straw bed, and neither saw nor heard anyone come or go.

Whenever he awoke there would be a plate of bread and a jug of water by his bedside. Sometimes the water would taste brackish and it would send him into a deep sleep. When he woke up, he would discover his hair had been cut and his nails trimmed.

Only once did he ever come into contact with another human being. A hand came around the door of his cell with a pen and a piece of paper. It guided him to write the three words which he had first shown the jailer: 'Reiter' and 'Caspar Hauser'.

One day some boots and an envelope were thrust into his hand and soon he found himself hobbling painfully through the centre of Nuremberg.

WILD RUMOURS

Caspar's story swept the taverns like wildfire. Suddenly he found himself the star of Nuremberg. The city council published a much-embellished account of Caspar's strange upbringing. It broadcast an appeal throughout the land for clues to his true identity. But many gossip-mongers and tittle-tattlers had already made up their minds who Caspar was. Some puritans said he was a child of the devil; mystics asserted that he had been sent from an alien planet; others were convinced Caspar was of royal birth.

There was certainly some circumstantial evidence for this last theory. In 1812, around the time that baby Caspar was dumped on the labourer's doorstep, the ruler of the province, Grand Duke Karl and the Grand Duchess Stephanie, had a baby son. But he died of meningitis - at least according to the doctors.

Had the true heir to the Grand Duke been spirited away at birth by rival claimants?

The couple had no more children, and when the Grand Duke died in 1829 the succession passed to the male line of the Countess of Hochberg. Only weeks after the Grand Duke's death, a year since Caspar's arrival in Nuremberg, an incident occured which seemed to support the theory.

AN ASSASSIN'S VICTIM

Casper arrived in Nuremberg, was now living at the home of Professor George Daumer, a respected philosopher and educationalist. In a short time the professor had transformed Caspar from a backward child into a bright, articulate young man, a prized guest in Nuremburg's drawing rooms.

One night the professor returned home to find Caspar lying in a pool of blood on the basement floor. He had been stabbed several times in the face and neck and was lucky to escape with his life. Caspar told the professor that a masked man had broken into the house and attacked him.

The gossips had a field day. This surely was the work of a would-be assassin hired by the Countess of Hochberg to do away with the rightful heir to the late Grand Duke's title.

Some people resented the acclaim being heaped upon Caspar. A waif with a mysterious upbringing was one thing, an interesting diversion at high society parties. A young man with pretensions to royalty was quite another. Some even whispered that he had faked the attack in the basement to surround himself with an even greater aura of mystery.

This band of cynics grew when, after the assault, the frightened Caspar was given a police guard at a secret address. The city was beginning to tire of the boy.

NEW 'PROTECTORS'

Then the eccentric English earl, Lord Stanhope arrived. He was fascinated by the remarkable story of the Child of Nuremberg, and managed to persuade the city council to allow him to become Caspar's legal guardian. In 1831, with Caspar in tow, he set off on a tour of the minor courts of Europe, parading the boy to the delight of dukes and princes.

But after two years on the road, the noble lord tired of his charge. Not for the first time in his wretched life Caspar was unceremoniously dumped. Lord Stanhope decided to lodge him with a mean-spirited puritan pastor named Meyer in the town of Ansbach, fifteen miles from Nuremberg. Caspar, now twenty-one, was put to work as an apprentice bookbinder, which he is said to have enjoyed.

THE MYSTERY REMAINS

One evening in December 1833, as he walked home from work through a park, Caspar was approached by a stranger who plunged a knife repeatedly into his ribs and ran off.

Mortally wounded, Caspar staggered to his lodgings where, incredibly, the

*Below: **The cradle that would have been Caspar's if the boy had been of royal birth. Was the child from nowhere really heir to the title of Grand Duke.***

pastor refused to believe his story. He accused Caspar of trying to gain attention by inflicting the wounds himself. Caspar was put to bed and the police were never called. Three days later, Caspar Hauser died in agony.

The pastor insisted that Caspar's terrible stab wounds were self-inflicted and did not call the police

---

The police found a black wallet near the scene of the crime. Inside was a note, in mirror writing: 'Hauser will be able to tell you who I am. To spare him the task I will tell you myself. I am from ... on the Bavarian border ... My name is MLO.' The assassin was never found.

Hearing of Caspar's death, the Grand Duchess Stephanie is reported to have broken down and wept, sobbing that she believed he was indeed her long-lost son.

Caspar was buried in the tiny country churchyard at Ansbach. His grave is still there to this day. The simple epitaph on his tombstone reads: 'Here lies Caspar Hauser, Enigma. His birth was unknown, his death mysterious.'

T.E. LAWRENCE
Arabian Sands

White-robed Lawrence of Arabia was one of the great heroes of World War I. What made this enigmatic man enlist in the ranks afterwards? And was his death in a motorcycle crash really an accident, or was he 'eliminated'?

The powerful Brough motorcycle accelerated through the winding lanes of the Dorset countryside. The rider enjoyed the sensation of speed, the almost sensual thrill of dicing with injury or death. In under a minute the machine

Right: *Lawrence of Arabia poses for the camera in Arab headgear and flowing robes. This was the image he wished to present to the world.*

Opposite: *An avid British public devoured every scrap of information about Lawrence. This photograph, which was captioned 'The Kingmaker', fed their adulation.*

Below: *Colonel Lawrence stands with other military dignitaries behind the Emir Feisal. Such local leaders used Lawrence's martial expertise to maintain power.*

Above: *Simple Bedouin Sheiks rallied to his call. Here Lawrence confers with a group of them as they outline their strategy in the sand.*

had roared the mile or so from his cottage to Bovington Army Camp.

The soldiers on the gate knew him well by sight. He greeted them, dismounted and walked to the camp post office to send a telegram inviting a friend from London to visit him the following day. He returned to his machine and headed back towards his cottage.

Just 400 yards from home the rider swerved to avoid two boy cyclists, hit the verge and somersaulted over the

Right: *Encamped in the desert with tents and camels...Lawrence's exploits became the stuff of legend. At the time he gloried in it.*

handlebars of his motorbike. Without a crash helmet he hit the road, fracturing his skull.

Six days later he died in the local hospital without fully regaining consciousness.

Thus ended the life of RAF Aircraftman Shaw, T. E., serial number 7875698. The hundreds of people who packed the tiny local church at Moreton for his funeral a week later, including generals, famous literary figures and even Winston Churchill, knew Shaw better as Colonel T.E. Lawrence - Lawrence of Arabia.

It was only the funeral of a low-ranking airman, but the church was packed with major public figures

---

The enigma of Thomas Edward Lawrence - to some a *Boys' Own* hero, leader of an Arab army and literary genius; to others a charlatan and a masochist - still divides historians today. Either way the legend survives.

His life inspired David Lean's epic film, *Lawrence of Arabia*. His death provoked a welter of theories, including murder and suicide.

OUT OF WEDLOCK

Lawrence was born in Tremadoc, Wales, in August 1888. His father, Thomas Chapman, an Irish landowner, had run off with the family nanny, Sarah Lawrence, taking her surname and leaving behind a wife, four daughters and most of his wealth. When T. E. was born to Sarah the family had to live on the comparatively modest income of £300 a year from Thomas's former estate.

The young Lawrence won a scholarship to Oxford University where he read history at Jesus College. One of Lawrence's tutors, Ernest Barker, got an insight into his student's character. He concluded that Lawrence's studies were merely 'a hurdle to be jumped on the road to action'.

On a research trip to France, he claimed, his sketches and maps got him mistakenly arrested as a spy. In his next year at Oxford he enrolled in the university shooting club and the Officer Cadet Training Corps. Lawrence's future was being shaped.

FAME AND ITS PRICE

By the outbreak of World War I, Lawrence was an expert on the Middle East. He had spent five years working on archaeological

Left: *Lawrence (left) in full desert robes, with colleague Lowell Thomas.*

Below: *One of Lawrence's own photographs of troops advancing in the desert with him. The original is in the Imperial War Museum, London.*

sites in Syria, the Lebanon and Palestine. He had also, it has recently been revealed, been part of a spying network on the progress of the Berlin to Baghdad railway being built by the Germans.

Excavating an archaeological site gave Lawrence a cover for spying on the German-built railway in Mesopotamia

---

Lawrence was in a group ostensibly funded by the British Museum to carry out a dig at Carchemish in Mesopotamia, now Iraq. He was armed with a camera and telephoto lens, while 'excavating' conveniently close to the railway line.

His almost unrivalled knowledge of the Arab world and its leaders meant that by 1916 Lawrence was appointed a special adviser to Sherif Feisal, who later became King of Iraq. Together they stirred up a rebellion against the Turks, allies of the Germans, in Arabia.

Lawrence's exploits are now the stuff of legend. Gradually discarding his British Army uniform for Arab garments, his armoured cars for camels, Lawrence led his 'Arab Army' against formidable Turkish opposition - and won.

He captured the key port of Aqaba on the Red Sea coast and cut a swathe through Turkish lines up to Damascus in Syria.

The personal cost to Lawrence was something which would affect the rest of his life. On a spying mission in the town

Below: *A smiling T.E. Lawrence, 'soldier and administrator', at British Headquarters in Cairo.*

Below right: *A rare unposed photograph in which he has not dressed for his role as an Arab military leader.*

After the war, and with Lawrence hailed as a hero - the gruesome details of his capture had by this stage not been made public - he became a special adviser on Arab affairs to Winston Churchill, who was chairman of a British Government Committee on the Middle East. With Churchill he attended the 1921 Cairo Conference, which established the new post–war order in the region.

DISAPPEARING INTO THE RANKS

The following year he wrote to his friend, the poet Robert Graves, that he wanted to become 'ordinary', to escape from his own fame and responsibilities. He then wrote to Air Marshall Sir Hugh Trenchard, Chief of the Air Staff, asking if he could enlist as an ordinary airman in the newly formed RAF. Trenchard was surprised, to say the least. But Lawrence's determination was so great that Trenchard eventually gave in and sent the following memo to his chief of RAF personnel:

'It is hereby approved that Colonel T. E. Lawrence be permitted to join the Royal Air Force as an Aircraft Hand under the alias of John Hume Ross. On receipt of any communication from him asking for his release, orders are to be issued for his discharge forthwith.' At least, if he didn't like it, Lawrence had a return ticket.

To his amazement, the legendary leader of the revolt in the desert was declared medically unfit for the RAF

When Lawrence arrived at the RAF recruiting office in London's Covent Garden two weeks later he was amazed when a medical officer decided he was unfit to serve. He had indeed spent the previous months sweating over his book, which had taken its toll, but Lawrence of Arabia unfit to be an ordinary airman? Finally, an officer who had been told of Lawrence's true identity took the medical officer to one side...and Colonel Lawrence became Air Hand Ross. He was posted to the air photography school at Farnborough in Kent.

But someone blew the whistle on

of Deraa, a key rail junction between Amman and Damascus, Lawrence was captured, whipped and apparently homosexually raped by the town's Turkish military governor, Hajim Bey, and his henchmen.

Captured by the Turks, Lawrence was first beaten and then homosexually raped by a group of soldiers

---

He wrote in his famous book *Seven Pillars of Wisdom*, that he was first whipped: 'The men took me up very deliberately, giving me "so many", and [would] then... ease themselves and play unspeakably with me.' He added: 'At last when I was completely broken they seemed satisfied.' With the ordeal over the corporal then kicked him. 'I remember smiling idly up at him, for a delicious warmth, probably sexual, was swelling through me,' he wrote.

Lawrence escaped from the evil Turks' clutches. But never from the torment, of both the pain and the pleasure which he had experienced.

Above: *Lawrence of Arabia's English retreat: Clouds Hill, Dorset, as seen from the Rhododendron Wood above the isolated cottage.*

Above: *One of the two bicycles that Lawrence swerved to avoid before his fatal motorcycle accident.*

Right: *Albert Hargreaves who was riding one of the bicycles escaped the accident unscathed.*

Opposite: *Idolized even beyond death...an effigy of Aircraftman Thomas Edward Shaw in his better-known role of Lawrence of Arabia.*

Airman Ross. the *Daily Express* broke the story on 27 December 1922: 'LAWRENCE OF ARABIA - FAMOUS WAR HERO BECOMES A PRIVATE' Three weeks later Lawrence discharged himself from the RAF.

Lawrence went back to his writing, but there was something about the discipline of the life of a 'squaddie' that he still yearned for. In March the following year, Lawrence changed his name to T. E. Shaw and joined the Tank Corps.

Lawrence realized that at the age of

thirty-three and with an upper-class accent he would not survive five minutes in a barrack room. So he took along with him an eighteen-year-old Scot called John Bruce as a 'minder'. Bruce later admitted that part of his job was to administer the birch to his master.

Lawrence took a young 'minder' into the Army with him - his duties included birching his employer

---

By early 1925 Lawrence had suffered enough at the hands of his Tank Corps brothers-in-arms and appealed to his well-placed friends at the Air Ministry to get him back into the Air Force. By this time, however, there was a Labour government, which regarded Lawrence as something of a snob and an imperialist. His request was refused.

HOUNDED BY THE PRESS

But in June that year an American magazine came out with a story headlined: 'LAWRENCE OF ARABIA - NEW DISGUISE' and revealed that he was now a private in the Tank Corps. The magazine also revealed details of his flogging in Deraa, without going into the more unsavoury parts of the incident. Lawrence was scared, and his old friend Sir Hugh Trenchard was moved enough to get him a job back in the RAF. Trooper Shaw of the Tank Corps now became Aircraftman Shaw of the RAF.

In his new disguise Lawrence was posted to India, probably to get him out of the way. He served first in Karachi and was then moved to defend an airstrip at Miranshah on the North West Frontier.

But again news leaked out. Amazing rumours reached governments all over the world that the famous Colonel Lawrence had been sent to India on a series of secret missions. He was stirring up an Afghan rebellion. He was spying on the Russians. He was, in fact, a war waiting to happen. Questions were asked in the House of Commons, and Lawrence's activities were front page news every other day.

In fact, Aircraftman Shaw was happily engaged in obeying his NCOs, guarding his airstrip on the North West Frontier and trying to write a book. But the scandal was too much for the British government. Lawrence was ordered home on the next boat out of Bombay.

There is no doubt that the incident made him many enemies both at home and abroad. The Russians, who had been trying to gain a foothold in northern India, were convinced that Lawrence was behind an Afghan uprising against Bolshevik influence in their country. At home many senior officials, both in the military and in the government, regarded the erstwhile hero as an embarrassment.

Lawrence remained in the ranks of the RAF until February 1935, tinkering with engines at a seaplane squadron on the south coast. The publication of *Seven Pillars of Wisdom* had brought him great literary acclaim. He left the RAF and took Cloud's Hill Cottage, set on a hill above Bovington Camp.

UNANSWERED RIDDLES

Many unanswered riddles surround his death. How could Lawrence, an experienced motorcyclist, crash while swerving to avoid two cyclists travelling in single file on the other side of the road? Who was driving a mystery black car which he is said to have swerved to avoid seconds before the crash?

The question of the car, spotted by a soldier from Bovington who was just yards from the accident, was discounted at the inquest, which was held with unprecedented haste on the morning of Lawrence's funeral. It is also fairly certain that Lawrence's vast experience and intellect were being used to help formulate a new policy to gear up the RAF to a war footing following German rearmament. Did the Germans know this and decide that Lawrence was too dangerous to live? Alternatively, had the Bolsheviks finally got their revenge for his alleged involvement in Afghanistan?

Indeed, had the British government itself decided that Lawrence now knew too much and could not be trusted?

Or had he finally succumbed to the pressure of his fame and the torment of his fascination with the whip? Did Lawrence of Arabia take his own life?

NOBLE ODDITIES
Foibles of the Rich

The British aristocracy has bred countless oddities from harmless eccentrics to dangerous lunatics. One Duke lived in underground tunnels like a mole. A famous society hostess believed she was Queen of the Jews. There was an Earl who dined in splendour, his dogs seated at table with him...

Money may not make you mad - but it has certainly had a stunning effect on the upper classes. Britain's eccentric aristocrats have had the millions to indulge their every bizarre whim - and the arrogance to ignore the stunned reactions of their fellow countrymen.

LORD ROKEBY.

*Above: **Lord Rokeby, whose holiday to a spa led him to become an 'amphibian'.***

*Opposite: **Wanting to wed the Messiah, Lady Hester Stanhope shunned London society.***

*Left: **The family of prime minister Lord North produced more than one eccentric.***

SENDING IT UP IN SMOKE

Sometimes their inheritance has literally gone up in smoke. Take the amazing case of the rebellious young grandson of Lord North, the eighteenth-century Prime Minister.

Resenting his family's background, he ran away from their country seat - Rougham Hall in Norfolk - and joined the navy. When his father died he returned home to claim his inheritance.

But the young Lord North packed the cellars of the Hall with the gunpowder, lit the fuse and destroyed the house.

THE UNDERGROUND ARISTOCRAT

But in one celebrated case the family fortunes went underground. William John Cavendish Bentinck Scott, the fifth Duke of Portland, was obsessively shy. He loathed meeting people, and visitors were barred from his home, Welbeck Abbey in Nottinghamshire.

The Duke decided there was only one thing to do: burrow. He built a series of subterranean rooms, including the largest ballroom in the country, a huge library and a billiard room that could house a dozen billiard tables. And like a human mole he linked his underground kingdom with fifteen miles of tunnels. One tunnel, a mile and a quarter long, connected his coachhouse with Worksop railway station.

In a black carriage with drawn blinds he would travel through the tunnel from Welbeck to the station. Still seated in the carriage he would be loaded into a railway truck. At his London home in Cavendish Square the servants would be sent out of sight as he climbed from the carriage and rushed into the privacy of his study.

Born in 1800, he spent his early years as a normal young man and he became an MP. But slowly his shyness took control of his mind. When the Duke moved into Welbeck he cleared the vast halls of their treasures and portraits and dumped them in a huge pile. He lived alone in five bare rooms in the west wing.

But if the Duke lived for most of his eighty years in the utmost privacy, in death he became a very public person in a bizarre court case. He had been buried simply and quietly in Kensal Green cemetery in North London. And soon, because of his mysterious lifestyle, the rumours of a double life began sweeping the capital.

Then up stepped a widow, Anna Maria Druce, who claimed that the dead Duke was really her late husband, Thomas, a shopkeeper. She swore that Thomas's funeral at Highgate cemetery had been a trick so that her husband, who had become disenchanted with his shopkeeper role, could return to his

reclusive role at Welbeck Abbey. The coffin, she said, had been empty - except for a hundredweight of lead. And she claimed the Portland title and all its lands. The case lasted for years but was dismissed when Thomas Druce's grave was ordered to be opened up, and there he lay.

THE WATER-LOVER

If the Duke of Portland would have preferred to be a mole, Lord Rokeby would have liked to be a toad. He believed that he should spend as much of his life as possible under water.

It was a holiday in the spa town of Aix-La-Chapelle that changed him from mammal to amphibian.

For years he had led the good life as one of the landed gentry of Kent. He came into the Rokeby title after the death

Below: *The poet Lord Byron was, of course, a genius as well as an eccentric. After years of wild living in England, he fled to the Continent where he carried on a series of steamy love affairs. He died nobly, however...in Greece, where he had gone to aid the cause of independence. He was just thirty-nine.*

given a half-crown to reward them for their excellent taste.

The water-loving aristocrat attempted to keep his strange obsession a secret. And in the end he built a vast swimming pool in his garden - covered by glass - where he would spend his day.

Lord Rokeby was a terrible embarrassment to his family, who feared him appearing in public displaying his strange habit of eating a leg of roast veal while immersed in the water.

His sister, Mrs Elizabeth Montagu dreaded that he might 'exhibit his amphibious and carnivorous habits at Bath'. She could not stand the thought of a 'gentleman's bathing with a loin of veal floating at his elbows'.

His strange habit of eating a leg of roast veal while swimming gave rise to rumours of cannibalism

---

Many thought he was a cannibal because of the meat that he ate while bobbing around in the water. His love of water obviously did the trick. He died at the grand old age of eighty-eight.

QUEEN OF THE JEWS

But there were aristocratic women who were eccentrics too. Lady Hester Stanhope, niece of Prime Minister William Pitt the Younger, was an extraordinary example.

An extremely attractive hostess in London society, she had one belief - that she was to be Queen of the Jews.

It was in 1810, when she was thirty-three that she left England to go and fulfil her destiny. Astrologers and fortune-tellers in London had assured her of her fate.

She set out on her voyage with a group of friends including a young man, Michael Bruce, who was to become her lover. Rumour has it that, when they reached Athens, Lord Byron dived off the rocks to greet her.

But soon after setting sail from Constantinople for Cairo they were shipwrecked close to the island of Rhodes. All their clothes were lost and Lady Hester opted to wear Turkish male

of an uncle who had been Bishop of Armagh and Primate of Ireland. The new Lord Rokeby was a picture of responsibility. But then came his foreign holiday to 'take the waters'.

Every day afterwards he would spend hours in the sea off the beaches of Kent. His servants had difficulty dragging him out on to dry land.

His favourite bathing place was on the sands of Hythe, three miles from his home at Mount Morris. His builders constructed a beach hut there for him. And he started to swim so much that he often fainted and had to be rescued.

He started to grow the most enormous beard. It hung down to his waist and was so thick and wide that it could be seen from behind.

He insisted on walking to the beach wearing peasant clothing. But behind him would come his carriage with a servant kitted out in the most splendid finery. If it rained the servant would ride in the carriage - but Lord Rokeby enjoyed getting soaking wet.

He had drinking fountains installed on the pathway so could always have his beloved water at hand. And if he came across anyone drinking at them they were

*Above: **When Lady Hester Stanhope tired of travel, she settled in a disused monastery near Sidon in Lebanon to await the new Messiah to claim her as his bride.***

*Above: **The eighth Earl of Bridgewater believed that nothing was too good for his pets, which were waited on by teams of servants.***

treated with great respect. Fascinated crowds poured coffee in front of her horse as she rode by, side-saddle, and in Jerusalem the doors of the Church of the Holy Sepulchre were thrown open to her.

She became more royal than royalty and began to think of herself as Queen Hester. After an historic voyage across the Arabian desert she was welcomed as queen of the desert and crowned.

But in 1914 she grew tired of her meanderings, settled down in a disused monastery near Sidon in Lebanon and waited for the new Messiah to come to claim her as his bride. She died penniless at the age of sixty-three, her pathetic dream as Queen of the Jews unfulfilled.

THE LORD WHO STAYED IN BED

The rich eccentric aristocrat can do anything he wants. Or nothing at all, as the new wife of Lord North discovered.

Their September wedding at Westminster was followed by a very successful Caribbean honeymoon. Returning to Burgholt House in October Lord North announced to his American bride that he was going to bed. 'That suits me just fine,' she said.

She was somewhat surprised the next day to find that she was up before he was. But dutifully she prepared his breakfast and took it up to him where he was not asleep but just lying there.

'You needn't have disturbed yourself,' said the butler. 'Breakfast in bed is already prepared for his Lordship. You see, October the ninth is the day on which he starts his hibernation.'

Shocked, she asked how long the hibernation lasted. 'Until March the twenty-second unless spring is very pleasant,' he replied. And he confirmed that Lord North spent all that time in bed. 'He just doesn't like the winter,' he added.

He ended: 'If you will forgive me, I must put the dining table in place.' When the amazed Lady North got upstairs she found their bedroom occupied a 25 ft Hepplewhite dinner table with a strangely cut hole towards one end. 'Sixteen to dinner tonight,' said the horizontal Lord North, 'and that's where I'll be sitting.' And he went on to explain.

clothing for the rest of her life.

They were rescued by a Royal Navy frigate and taken to Cairo, and so started an extraordinary series of adventures in the Middle East. Money was no object. Lady Hester played the part of an enormously wealthy haughty princess. The saddle of her horse was covered in crimson velvet inlaid with gold.

When all her clothing was lost in a shipwreck Lady Hester decided to wear Turkish male garb for the rest of her life

---

Some thought she was a boy because they could not understand how a woman could break all the rules of the Middle East. But she didn't care about rules, and broke them with such style that she was

'You see, my dear, no North has got out of bed from October to March since my ancestor lost the American colonies. Perhaps if he had hibernated as well, we might have been able to go on ordering you Yankees about instead of having to marry you.'

FOUR-LEGGED DINNER GUESTS

Francis Henry Egerton, the 8th Earl of Bridgwater, had no time for women. Or for his fellow men for that matter. He much preferred the company of his dogs. Nothing was too good for them. He even bought them the finest soft leather boots to protect their paws.

For if the Earl's first obsession was his dogs, his love of boots and shoes ran a very close second. He wore a new pair every day of the year. And when he kicked them off at night he ranged them around the walls and used them as a calendar.

His dogs were his only friends and every day he took half a dozen of them for rides in his carriage. Then at night he would dine with them in the great hall.

The huge table would be laid for twelve and his dogs would be led in - with crisp white napkins around their necks. Servants stood behind their chairs to dish out their food on to the family silver. The Earl would engage them in conversation as if they were friends and relatives. To cynics who commented on his madness the Earl would reply that his dogs were better behaved than any gentleman.

The Earl lived for many years in Paris, where he upset his neighbours by his shooting habits.

As his eyesight grew worse he would clip the wings of pigeons and use them for easy target practice.

Baron De Rothschild's superb chateau in Buckinghamshire was home to many creatures great and small. In the 1860s guests could expect to be driven up the long drive in a carriage drawn by four zebras.

Inside snakes writhed around the bannisters, and a supposedly tame bear had a habit of slapping women guests on the bottom. But the most amazing incident in the Baron's animal kingdom happened in the 1890s at an important political dinner for Lord Salisbury.

A tame bear had the habit of slapping female guests on the behind

Seated around the the long table each of the twelve guests noticed that there was an empty chair beside them. Obviously their dinner neighbours were

Below: *Sir Lionel Walter, the second Baron Rothschild, would transport guests in a carriage drawn by four zebras*

late in arriving. Suddenly the great doors at the end of the dining room opened, and in walked twelve immaculately dressed monkeys to take up the spare seats.

THE MANIAC BUILDER

Mega-rich William Beckford had a very different type of obsession - his foible was building tall spires that promptly crashed to the ground. And he had no shortage of cash to satisfy his ambitions.

At the age of ten when his father died in 1770, he inherited £1 million in cash and property in England. Not to mention large sugar plantations in Jamaica. His investment income was £100,000 a year - an absolute fortune in those days.

Beckford did everything in a hurry. Highly intelligent he wrote books in a couple of days. As he said after finishing one novel in French: 'I never took off my clothes for three days and nights. This severe application made me very ill.'

He travelled widely and was particularly impressed by the giant spires he saw on religious buildings in Spain and Portugal. And when after a disastrous marriage he settled at his family estate in 1795, they became the examples that he intended to emulate. At Fonthill he planned an enormous Gothic abbey, a private folly with a vast tower as its centrepiece. Beckford boasted that he was going to have the highest private home in Britain. But first he built a wall

Top left: *William Beckford inherited a fortune and spent it in a hurry building edifices that did not even survive him.*

Above: *Author William Beckford maintains a moonlit vigil over the madcap building work at Fonthill. But his vast Gothic abbey turned a costly folly.*

seven miles long and 12 ft high around the estate to keep out inquisitive eyes. Then he started in earnest - and in a rush. He couldn't wait for proper foundations to be dug. He decided, against his builder's advice, that the foundations that had been dug for a smaller house would be satisfactory. He used cement and wood instead of stone and brick because they were quicker to work with.

Five hundred labourers were employed, with one shift working by torchlight through the night. He even poached 450 building workers away from work on St George's Chapel at Windsor when he estimated that things were going too slowly. But he gave them too much beer as a bribe to work faster, and most of the time they worked on the great tower blinded by ale.

He demanded the use of every cart and

wagon in the area - much to the frustration of local farmers. After six years the great building was complete. The magnificent spire soared to 300 ft above the beautiful abbey.

But then the first gale blew. The spire literally snapped in two and hurtled to the ground. Coolly, millionaire Beckford announced that he was sorry he hadn't seen it crashing down - and gave orders for a new tower to be started immediately.

Seven years later the new tower was finished. But this time he had used stone to give it strength. Inside the dazzlingly decorated abbey he lived a bizarre life alone with one servant - a Spanish dwarf. But every day his dining table was set for twelve. And the cooks would be ordered to prepare food for twelve.

On his first Christmas in the newly built abbey he said he would only eat Christmas dinner if it was cooked in new

kitchens. His builders told him it was not possible to finish them in time. But that wasn't any answer for the eccentric aristocrat.

On Christmas Day the fires were lit in the ovens. The mortar was hardly dry, the bricks had not settled and the timbers were not securely fixed. Dinner was in due course served. But as the small army of servants cleared the plates a crash reverberated around the abbey. The new kitchens had collapsed.

In 1822, after a slump in sugar prices, Beckford was forced to sell his dream folly to an ammunition dealer, John Farquhar, for £330,000. But the new owner did not get a good deal. Within months of his arrival the giant spire came crashing down again.

Beckford moved to Bath, but was disappointed to find that his new home was missing one essential - a tower. He promptly built one, but made sure that it was a mere 130 ft high. The great folly builder died in 1844 aged eighty-four. And for once his tower outlived him. It is still there today.

THE DRESSED UP LORD

Lord Cornbury, the 3rd Earl of Clarendon, was Queen Anne's cousin. And she gave him the plum job of representing her as Governor of New York and Jersey in America.

But he took it all a little too seriously. As he told friends: 'In this place I represent a woman, and in all respects I ought to represent her faithfully.' This was his excuse for turning up at the opening of the New York Assembly in 1702 in a blue silk gown and satin shoes, and carrying a fan.

He loved to show off on the streets wearing a hooped skirt, but his long-suffering wife did not have such a happy time. All his money went on his clothes, and he gave her none for hers. She was forced to resort to stealing.

He was ordered to return to England in 1708 to pay his debts but stayed a favourite of Queen Anne.

And he didn't change his habits upon his return, he was spotted in Worcestershire 'in a gown, stays, tucker, long ruffles and cap'.

Below: When the Earl of Clarendon, Viscount Cornbury was sent by his cousin Queen Anne to represent her as Governor of New York, he arrived in America dressed as a woman.

CHILD PRODIGIES
Infants Who Amaze

What creates a Mozart, composing music when most children cannot write their own names? How can an illiterate peasant child perform complicated mental arithmetic at speed? For centuries child prodigies have fascinated scientists and public alike

Child prodigies have been astounding society for centuries with their amazing, almost magical abilities to understand things beyond the comprehension of even the most intelligent professors, maestros and theorists. These young wonders, who are literally one in a million, can solve the most complex mathematical problems, compose intricate symphonies, quote extensive passages of literature - and all before they reach their teens.

Zerah Colburn, for instance, took just four seconds to calculate how many seconds there were in eleven years.

Above: *Possibly the greatest composer who ever lived Wolfgang Amadeus Mozart playing the piano accompanied on the violin by his father.*

Opposite: *George Bidder was known in his youth as 'a calculating boy'. He grew up to become a renowned civil engineer.*

Left: *The English Methodist divine and hymn writer Charles Wesley. He was a musical prodigy who played harpsichord at the age of three.*

Wolfgang Amadeus Mozart could play the violin and piano brilliantly at the age of three. Arthur Greenwood knew the alphabet when he was just twelve months.

But these unique gifts do not come without their costs. Many prodigies had their brief day of fame, only to disappear from view, and never to fulfil their early expectations. Others died young. In many cases, the infant wonders were literally worked to death by over eager parents who hoped to cash in on their stunning talents, never allowing their offspring the time to explore the simple pleasures of youth.

Child genius is far more common in boys than in girls, probably because infantile gland disorders - thought to be responsible for creating the amazing talents - are mainly found in males. Medical authorities believe prodigies produce an exceptional level of hormones in certain glands, including the pituitary and adrenal. These child wonders, then, peak at an early age because their nervous systems reach their pinnacle long before the rest of their bodies develop.

Although some prodigies have graced the world of literature and fine art, they are extremely rare, experts say, and usually burn out quickly. Englishwoman Daisy Ashford was one. When she wrote *The Young Visiters* (sic) at the age of nine it was hailed as a masterpiece. She never came close to matching its brilliance.

Rather, young geniuses seem to excel in the fields of maths and music - because neither of those disciplines requires experience of life.

MUSICAL GENIUSES

Though a vast majority of child wonders fade into oblivion after a brief blaze of glory, musical child prodigies, many descended from eminent musical families, fare better because their works often live on.

The greatest of these was Mozart, arguably the finest composer who ever lived. Receiving practically his entire education from his father Leopold, himself a fine musician, the young Wolfgang was just three years old when he first became an attraction in Salzburg. By the time he was four, he could remember every note in every solo of the concertos he heard and liked.

His reputation as a musical genius soon brought him to the attention of the Austrian Emperor, and by the time he was six he, his father and sister Maria Anna, herself an accomplished pianist at the age of eight, embarked on a lengthy tour of Europe, playing for the crowned heads and aristocracy of several countries. Everywhere they went, Wolfgang caused a sensation with his exquisite touch - whether it was on the piano, violin or organ.

Despite the boy's amazing gifts, however, Wolfgang's father could not secure him an appointment equal to his status and talent. So, at the age of twenty-five, Mozart decided to try for himself.

Above: *Polish pianist and composer Frederick Chopin first performed for an audience at the age of only eight.*

Below: *Dr Richard Strauss, his wife and grandson. Strauss composed music from the age of six right up until his death.*

He left Salzburg for Vienna, where the following year he married a singer named Constanze Weber.

The marriage took its toll on Mozart's finances, which were meagre, but even when he was in the grip of poverty he continued to compose some of the most beautiful music the world has ever heard. In fact he left more than six hundred works. Within a few hours of his death, at the age of thirty-five in 1791, he was still working on his unfinished Requiem.

He was once asked to explain by a friend how he composed his sonatas and symphonies. Mozart replied, much to his friend's surprise, that he had no idea.

'When I am in particularly good condition, perhaps riding in a carriage, or in a walk after a good meal, and in a sleepless night, then the thoughts come to me in a rush and best of all,' he said.

'Whence or how - that I do not know and cannot learn: those which please me, I retain in my head and hum them perhaps to myself - at least, so others have told me. Then it goes on and I keep on expanding it and making it more distinct and the thing, however long it be, becomes almost finished in my head.'

Charles Wesley, nephew of the founder of Methodism, was another musical prodigy. Like Mozart, he showed an uncanny talent at the tender age of three

by playing for his startled father a tune on the harpsichord.

His genius quickly developed to the extent that, whenever he heard a tune or melody on the street, he would race home and play it - even though he never

studied music. When he was just four his father introduced him to the leading musicians of his day in eighteenth century London, and two years later he was being tutored by a master in Bristol.

Young Charles became so adept at playing the works of Handel and Scarlatti that at the age of twelve he was regarded as the most accomplished interpreter of their works in the world. He went on to enrich the musical world with many hymn tunes of his own.

When asked by a friend to explain how he composed music, Mozart replied that he had no idea

---

There were, of course, many other precocious musical prodigies. Chopin made his public debut when he was eight. Weber was appointed conductor of the Opera at Breslau when he was seventeen. Richard Strauss was composing music from the age of six and continued until his death. Haydn too composed from the age of six. Sir Yehudi Menuhin was playing the violin with ease by the time he was three and at thirty-two was

Above: *Franz Josef Haydn composed from the age of six. Here his nautical experience inspires his great works:* **The Four Seasons** *and* **The Creation.**

Left: *British conductor Sir Ronald Landon, born in 1873, could play the piano before he could even talk.*

considered a virtuoso. And Sir Landon Ronald could play the piano before he could even talk.

Not all great young talents are remembered by history, however. One of the most remarkable reports of a musical prodigy appeared in the *Encyclopedia of Psychic Science*. It told of Blind Tom, a five-year-old black child, the son of slaves, dazzling pre-Civil War America by playing two tunes on the piano at the same time - one with each hand - while he sang a third!

YOUNG MATHEMATICIANS

Still, providence was on the whole far kinder to musical prodigies than to those who excelled in mathematics. Most of the latter faded into obscurity once their moment of glory passed.

Ampère, the great French physicist and mathematician whose name is now used to measure electric current, is a notable exception - for many reasons.

Not only did he achieve lasting fame and recognition, but he also showed amazing talents in more than one discipline. A voracious reader, he raced through every book his father could get him, but loved nothing better than devouring a twenty-one-volume encyclopedia - most of which he could recite verbatim many years later.

In 1786, when he was just eleven, he was already studying advanced mathematics. Within seven years he had mastered the intricate complexities of Lagrange's landmark publication, *Mechanique Analytique*.

During the remainder of his life - he died in 1836 - Ampère revolutionized mathematics, discovered the fundamental laws of electrodynamics and wrote important papers on chemistry, poetry and psychology.

Carl Friedrich Gauss, born in 1777 to a poor German family, is also remembered. At the age of twenty-four he published his *Disquisitiones Arithmetica*, which is considered a milestone in numerical theory.

Regarded as the premier mathematician of the nineteenth century, Gauss showed his promise amazingly early when, at the age of two, he mentally corrected his father's mistakes when working out the

Above: *Andrè Marie Ampère, the French physicist and mathematician whose name is now used as a measure of electric current. He could recite an encyclopedia verbatim.*

wages of some workmen. The boy became a local celebrity in his home town of Braunschweig and, thanks to some kindly noblemen, was given the chance to attend school, mastering the classical languages by the time he was eleven.

But maths was his real forte. Once a new mathematics teacher told him not to bother coming to lessons, because he couldn't teach him anything he didn't already know. By the time he was fourteen, he had been called to the court of the Grand Duke of Brunswick, where he entertained the aristocracy with his amazing memory and astonishing speed at solving difficult calculations.

But even Ampère and Gauss were no match for some of the most amazing mathematical prodigies, even if the latter following problems, which he solved in mere seconds, and always in his head - and remember, he could not perform even the most simple multiplication on paper.

Given that the distance between Boston and Concord is 65 miles, how many paces must it take, assuming each step is three feet? The answer, 114,400, was given in ten seconds.

What number multiplied by itself will produce 998,001? In less than four seconds he answered: 999.

While able to solve intricate mathematical problems at lightning speed in his head, he could not do the simplest sum on paper

---

Colburn's fame soon spread to Europe, and in 1812 his father took him to England, where the greatest mathematicians of the day quizzed him. The young prodigy answered every question correctly, and so quickly that the man appointed to take down the results had to ask him to slow down.

For instance, when asked the square root of 106,929 he answered '327' immediately - before the poor note-taker could even record the original figure! They tried another. What is the cube root of 268,336,125? Without a second's thought, he replied '645'.

In another incredible feat, he proved that the number 4,294,967,297 was not a prime number - one that could only be divided by 1 and itself - even though it had long been asserted that it was. In his head, he worked out that the number was equal to 641 x 6,700,417.

Give the square of 999,999? Answer: 999,998,000,001. In five seconds, he worked out the cube root of 413,993,348,677 (7453).

The questions kept coming. How many times would a coach wheel, 12 feet in circumference, turn around in 256 miles. And how many minutes are there in 48 years? He answered both in less than four seconds. To the amazement of everyone present, with the second of these two answers he gave the number of seconds as well!

Inexplicably, within two years of his dramatic performance before the great

Zerah Colburn
Aged 8 years.
Remarkable for solving Arithmetical questions.
Copied by permission from the original.
Pub. April 7 1813, by R. S. Kirby, n London House Yard, St Pauls

never fully bloomed into greatness. Zerah Colburn, for example, lost his powers of calculation when he was just ten, but his wondrous feats still amaze. Born in Vermont in 1804, Colburn had no mathematical education, and yet by the time he was six was giving public demonstrations of his skills. Consider the

Above: *Zerah Colburn at the age of eight was asked 'How many minutes are there in 48 years?' He answered correctly in four seconds.*

minds of Europe he lost his amazing powers entirely. As a young man he tried his hand at acting, but failed, so in 1821 he returned to America where he was ordained a deacon in the Methodist Church. For the next fourteen years he served as an itinerant preacher until appointed as a language professor to a small seminary college. He died at the age of thirty-five.

The young prodigy answered the questions so quickly that the note-taker had to ask him to slow down

---

One of the greatest English child prodigies was George Bidder, who was born in Moretonhampstead, Devon in 1805. Billed as the 'Calculating Boy', Bidder showed extraordinary abilities at

Below: *Philosopher John Stuart Mill in a photograph taken in 1860.*

the age of four, even though he could not even count to ten until he was six! Nor could he read figures, and his command of language was so poor that he did not even know there was such a word as 'multiply'.

But he so dazzled everyone who met him that his father took him on a tour of England, and soon everyone was clamouring to see the 'Calculating Boy' who answered every poser with consummate ease:

What is the compound interest on £4444 for 4444 days at 4 1/2 per cent per annum? In two minutes, he gave the answer: £2434, 16 shillings and 5 1/4 pence.

How long does it take to fill a cistern with a volume of one cubic mile at the rate of 120 gallons per minute? Again in two minutes came the reply: 14,300 years, 285 days, 12 hours and 46 minutes. Bidder even took leap years into account!

If a clock pendulum vibrates the distance of 9 3/4 inches in a second, how many inches will it vibrate in 7 years, 14 days, 2 hours, 1 minute and 56 seconds, if each year is precisely 365 days, 5 hours, 48 minutes and 55 seconds? In less than a minute, Bidder replied 2,165,625,744 3/4 in.

If a flea jumps 2 ft 3 in in every leap, how many hops would it take to go around the world, whose circumference is 25,020 miles? And how long would it take, given that it hops once every second without a break. In seconds, the answers came: 58,713,600 leaps, and 1 year, 314 days, 13 hours and 20 minutes.

Bidder, who eventually spent some time in school and was then privately tutored, rose to great heights, becoming one of England's greatest engineers. He was largely responsible for founding the London telegraph system, constructed the Victoria Docks, and became the President of the Institution of Civil Engineers.

His amazing powers actually increased with time, and in problems where some special properties played a role he was equalled only by Ampère.

Two days before his death, in 1878, a friend posed the following problem. Given that the speed of light is 190,000 miles a second, and the wavelength of the red rays is 36,918 to the inch, how many of its waves must strike the eye in one second? As his friend pulled out a pencil to calculate the answer, Bidder reportedly replied: 'You need not work it out. The number of vibrations will be 444,433,651,200,000.'

Unusually for a former child genius, George Bidder retained his amazing abilities until he died in his seventies

---

Unfortunately, history has not always recorded the exploits of prodigies so well as those listed above. Nevertheless, enough remains of their legendary abilities for even twentieth-century men and women to admire their genius.

Miguel Mantilla, a Mexican-born infant, was just two years old when he could answer questions like: 'In what years did, or will, 4 February be a Friday?' He could rattle off the answers in less than ten seconds.

George Watson, a native of Buxted in Sussex, was born in 1785. He was considered almost an idiot in everything except calculation and memory. Although he could neither read nor write, he performed in his head the most difficult mathematical problems and could answer correctly, without hesitation, any questions concerning what day of the week it was for any date in history. If the date happened to be during his lifetime, he could also say where he was and what the weather had been. He could also describe and count every church and public house in every village, town and city throughout the neighbouring counties.

Some prodigies have exhibited all-round amazing skills. Christian Heinecken, who was known as the 'Infant of Lubeck', startled everyone in Germany when, a few hours after his birth in 1721, he began talking. Before he was a year old, it is reported that he could remember all the major events in the first five books of the Old Testament. And by his second birthday he could name all the historical happenings in the Bible, as well as knowing Latin, French and geography.

John Stuart Mill, the nineteenth century philosopher and economist, could read Greek at the age of three. By the time he was ten was completely at ease with the complex works of Plato and Demosthenes.

Thomas Macaulay was one of England's all-round geniuses. At seven he had already written a universal history, at eight composed a thesis on how to convert the natives in Malabar to Christianity, and at fourteen he could recite all of Milton's 'Paradise Lost'.

Blaise Pascal, the French philosopher and mathematician, was likewise an all-round wonder child. Before he was twelve, he was writing theses on acoustics, and he invented the first calculating machine at nineteen. By the time of his thirtieth birthday, just nine years before his death in 1662, he had written several books on religion.

Today eleven-year-old Ganesh Sittampalam, who lives in Surbiton, Surrey, could well lay claim to being the world's smartest child. He's already the youngest university student on the planet, and is currently speeding through his course even though he only attends lectures once a week. At his present pace, he should have his Bachelor of Science degree by the time he's thirteen.

Above: *Blaise Pascal was a seventeenth-century French mathematician and religious philosopher.*

STAR FOLLIES
'Showbiz' Shockers

Voracious sexual appetites, dangerous practical jokes, black magic rituals and a terrible fear of growing up - hallmarks of some of the freaky superstars of twentieth-century showbusiness

With more money than sense, the glitzy stars of showbiz and pop enjoy themselves with a vengeance. Cash is the last thing on their minds when they set out to indulge their eccentricities. Bizarre, freaky, wild, sexy or just plain daft, the household names of screen and record often outperform their screen characters in their own lives.

KEITH MOON

The drummer with the Who rock group was a lunatic on stage - and off it. On stage he regularly wrecked his drum kit. Off stage he thought nothing of

Opposite: Greta Garbo was the ultimate sex symbol...mysterious, unattainable, who always wanted to 'be alone'.

Below left: Rolling Stone Mick Jagger has a pretty good line in eccentricity himself - but he also once suffered at the hands of Keith Moon. Moon interrupted his honeymoon night with Bianca.

Below: The Who's drummer Keith Moon started his day with two bottles of champagne before tackling a couple of bottles of brandy.

wrecking his car by driving it into a swimming pool.

Whenever he stayed in hotels he went on orgies of destruction. He dropped firecrackers down the loo, blowing holes in the floor. He chopped furniture into firewood and threw TVs out of the window. He earned a fortune - but spent it before he could count it.

The clown's antics in hotels cost him £200,000! He explained his bizarre behaviour simply: 'The momentum is still there when I come off stage. I'm like an express train or an ocean liner. It takes me two or three miles to stop.'

Moon was like a child who could permanently misbehave and knew he would never be punished. His cash would always protect him. When asked what he feared most, he replied: 'Having to grow up.'

Born in August 1947, the son of a London motor mechanic, he moved from job to job until he joined The Who in the 1960s. He got an audition with the group

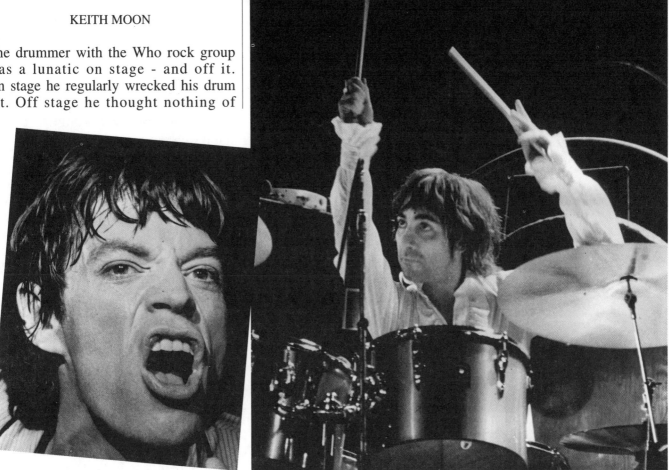

simply by saying that he was a better drummer than the one they had. Lead singer Roger Daltrey remembered that Moon turned up with orange hair and wearing an orange suit. They called him the Gingerbread Man.

He ended the audition by smashing up his drum kit. It was to become his trademark at concerts worldwide. Moon became known as the wild man of pop.

He started the day with a Bucks Fizz - champagne and orange juice - out of a mug, lying back in a black velvet, monogrammed dressing-gown. It was just a warm-up for his daily intake of two bottles of champagne and a couple of bottles of brandy. And then the fun started. Moon didn't care who were the victims of his pranks. Mick Jagger exploded with rage after Moon ruined a honeymoon night after the Stone's wedding to Bianca. The couple were asleep in their eleventh floor hotel room in Hollywood when they heard movement on their balcony. Mick took a gun from under his pillow and aimed it at the curtains.

Suddenly they were swept aside and

there was Moon. 'Good evening,' he said. The madcap pop star had climbed from balcony to balcony, hundreds of feet up, to offer his wedding congratulations.

When Moon blew up his drum kit on stage with gunpowder, Bette Davis fainted in the wings

---

His antics were often explosive. On American TV Moon decided that The Who's performance would end with a bang. He arranged for a special effects man to blow up his drum kit with gunpowder. Unfortunately Moon kept on plying him with drink. And with every drink more and more gunpowder was poured into the explosive device.

The result was dramatic. Moon was thrown backwards through the scenery. Lead guitarist Pete Townsend stood petrified, his hair ablaze. And when Moon lurched forward out of the scenery to take his bow he was covered in blood, with pieces of drum kit embedded in his arms. Screen star Bette Davis, who had been watching from the wings, promptly fainted with shock.

Dressing up was another of his favourite pranks. The police were not amused when they got involved in one of his stunts. A Rolls-Royce had drawn up in London's Oxford Street. Two huge but smart, obvious villains jumped out and leaped on an innocent-looking, middle-aged clergyman.

They gave him a kicking and beating worthy of the East End.The crowds on the pavements did nothing while the vicar was dragged screaming and kicking into the back of the Rolls. He was heard to yell: 'Have you no respect for the cloth?'

Two youths eventually gave chase and, seeing the vicar pinned in the back, called the police. When stopped at a roadblock, out stepped the vicar, unharmed. It was Keith Moon.

'I love to make people laugh,' he said. The police didn't.

In the mid-seventies after years of living in an alcoholic haze, Moon tried to cut back on drink with the help of fellow drummer Ringo Starr. But he still managed to get himself kicked off a British Airways jet after trying to break into the pilot's cabin demanding to play his drumsticks on the control panel.

One night in 1978 he went to a party and announced his engagement to blonde Swedish model Annette Walter-Lax. Next morning he was found dead of natural causes. He'd always said that he was going to die young. He was thirty-one.

ERROL FLYNN

A generation earlier, film star Errol Flynn was the swashbuckling hell-raiser who set new standards in showbiz for eccentricity - and scandalous behaviour. He designed himself a house of pleasure in the Hollywood Hills - a fortress for erotic amusements. The kinky Flynn even installed two-way mirrors in the ceilings of the bedroom so that he and his friends could observe his guests making love.

Flynn said of the visitors to Mulholland House: 'Strange people wended their way up the hill. Among them pimps, sports, bums, down-at-the-heel actors, queers, athletes, sightseers, process-servers, phonies, salesmen, everything in the world.' And of course, pretty girls.

In the later 1930s Flynn had taken over the role of handsome film hero John Barrymore. Said producer Jack Warner: 'He had mediocre talent, but to the Walter Mittys of the world he was all the heroes in one magnificent sexy animal package... actor or no actor, he showered an audience with sparks when he laughed, when he fought or when he loved.'

Flynn may have made the perfect screen Robin Hood. In real life he was a drunk with brittle bones and permanent piles. But he had an image to keep up as a rake. And he set about living up to it with spirit - mainly Scotch whisky. But his disgraceful philandering was to catch up with him in 1943. He was charged with rape after complaints from two Hollywood groupies, Betty Hansen and Peggy Satterlee.

Below: *Errol Flynn was a disgraceful philanderer. But his amorous activities rebounded in 1943 when he was charged with rape.*

Betty alleged that Flynn had raped her at a sex-and-swim party, while Peggy said that they had made love on the *Sirocco* in front of every porthole. Betty told how Flynn had undressed to have sex with her - but had kept his socks on. This caused some amusement amongst film-goers of the day. Flynn's last film had been *They Died with Their Boots On*. After the reputations of the two 'victims' had been destroyed by Flynn's lawyer, the jury had no difficulty acquitting him.

From the early 1950s it was downhill all the way. Drink and drugs pushed Flynn towards an early death.

JIMMY PAGE

While Errol Flynn built his house of pleasure Led Zeppelin guitarist Jimmy Page bought his dream home, which more accurately should be described as

Below: *How Aleister Crowley saw himself. This self-portrait of the man who called himself 'The Beast'.*

the House of a Thousand Nightmares. It had previously been owned by the character known as the Wickedest Man in the World.

Boleskine House, overlooking Loch Ness in Scotland, had been owned by Aleister Crowley, the English public schoolboy who became the King of Satanism. He was known as the Great Beast, 666, or the English Beelzebub.

Page, an authority on Satanism, was so obsessed that he bought Crowley's former temple, a brooding, sinister place haunted by the ghost of a man beheaded there. But the evil vibrations of the house and Page's dabbling with black magic had a deadly effect. It was as though Led Zeppelin had angered the devil, and it was cursed.

Heavy rock band Led Zeppelin were formed in 1968 after Jimmy Page's group the Yardbirds collapsed. Within a couple of years they had taken America and Europe by storm. In the seventies they were outselling the Rolling Stones albums by three to one. And indulging in the sex and drugs which went with success in the rock 'n' roll world.

Sex and drugs were also the keys to the working of Aleister Crowley's evil mind. Through them he sought a higher plateau of gratification.

But heroin and booze were taking their toll. Bonham was so chronic an alcoholic that a doctor had to travel with him. And then the run of bad luck started.

In August 1975 the car carrying Plant, his wife Maureen, their children and Jimmy Page's daughter crashed into a tree on the Greek island of Rhodes. Maureen fractured her skull, her husband broke an ankle and elbow, and the children fractured various limbs. Plant could not walk for six months.

Had Page's dabblings in black magic caused an awful curse to be laid on him and the members of Led Zeppelin?

The rumours began about Satan's curse on Led Zeppelin. At Boleskine House a caretaker had killed himself. And the man who replaced him went mad. In July 1977 a freak respiratory complaint killed Plant's five-year-old son Karac. Had

Jimmy Page upset his evil masters, and were they hitting back?

The final blow came in September 1980 when John Bonham was rehearsing at Page's other home at Windsor. On his way he dropped into a pub for lunch. With his sandwiches he drank sixteen vodkas. At the rehearsal, which turned into a party, he drank vodka after vodka until he collapsed in a coma. He never woke up. He was thirty-one.

The original Led Zeppelin would never play again. Had the Wickedest Man in the World returned for his final evil revenge?

GRETA GARBO

Movie star Greta Garbo was the ultimate recluse, mysterious, unattainable, a superstar who valued her privacy more than all the money in the world. She announced, 'I want to be alone,' and for the last forty years of her life she did not make a film.

Instead she became a legend, an enigma living a lonely life in Manhattan on the riches she had earned during her twenty-year Hollywood career.

She had an ex-directory phone number and even those who had it were always answered with 'Miss Garbo isn't in' by the ex-actress. She rarely went out. When she did, she flitted around the streets like a beautiful ghost. Her eyes were always shielded by dark glasses, and a slouching coolie-style straw hat covered most of her pale face.

Even in her death she insisted on being mysterious. Officials at New York Hospital, where she had been on a kidney dialysis machine, said it had been her wish that no details should be given.

She was very rich but very mean. When she went out to buy clothes it was at a sale, and she even sold back to the newsagent magazines she had bought and which she found on inspection to be without interest. In her last interview she said: 'I don't want any kind of attention from anybody, except that I know that someone likes me. Otherwise it's sickening.'

She was born Greta Lovisa Gustafsson in Stockholm, Sweden on 18 September, 1905, daughter of an uneducated labourer who was often ill or unemployed. She

left school at fourteen to help pay for his medical treatment, and vowed then to build her life so that she would never be financially dependent on anyone.

She began making her living in a barber shop, lathering men's faces. Her big break came at seventeen in the hat section of the department store where she then worked, when she was chosen to appear in a filmed hat advertisement. The stage-struck youngster enrolled at Stockholm's Royal Dramatic Theatre and haunted film studios seeking work.

Her career took off when Maurice Stiller, then Sweden's leading director, became besotted by the tall, angular beauty. He made her his protegee, changed her name to Garbo and starred her in his 1924 silent movie *The Atonement of Gosta Berling.*

She had light brown hair and greyish green eyes, and always kept her Swedish accent - which meant she could never pronounce her Ws. Said Hollywood director George Cukor: 'She could let an audience know she was thinking things

Top: *Greta Lovisa Gustafsson was the daughter of an uneducated and often unemployed Swedish labourer. Later she was to haunt film studios seeking work.*

Above: *The haunting beauty of Garbo... 'She could let an audience know she was thinking things and thinking them uncensored'.*

Above: Michael Jackson was a superstar before he even reached his teens. He has since been making up for his lost childhood.

getting into his stride when the Swedish actress suddenly pushed him away and leaped out of bed. She then proceeded to perform energetic aerobic exercises while singing an obscure Scandinavian peasant song.

When her bewildered lover asked her what she was doing, Garbo explained that it was her mother's tried and tested method of avoiding getting pregnant. It obviously worked for Garbo.

Garbo stopped making films in 1941 at the grand age of thirty-five. In her films she had always played ladies of mystery. Now she started playing the part in real life. The eccentric enigma spurned her adoring public totally and locked herself away in an apartment on East 52nd Street, New York. It was furnished in bare Swedish functional style with a few valuable paintings, Renoirs and Modiglianis. A cleaning lady came twice a week; otherwise she had her wish: she was alone until her death in 1990.

MICHAEL JACKSON

Megastar singer Michael Jackson did not have a childhood. He was a star by the age of ten. But he's been making up for it ever since.

As a child he was so busy singing that he never visited a zoo. So now he's bought himself one. Chimpanzee Bubbles is his favourite animal - Michael treats him like the child he so badly wants. The private zoo also boasts a giraffe called Mahali, snakes, llamas and peacocks.

He wanted a fire engine. So Wacko Jacko spent $150,000 on one for his ranch in the Santa Ynez valley, California. He wanted a train set. So he paid $7 million for a home which has its own railway track running up to the front door from the tennis courts.

In the past fifteen years he has undergone over a dozen operations and paid plastic surgeons more than $250,000 to transform his image. He has spent $90,000 on a pressurized oxygen chamber so that he can breathe pure air at his home. He takes regular naps in it, so that he can live to be 150.

For exercise he dances for hours, copying the movements of his animals for new dance steps. Said Jerome

and thinking them uncensored.'

Garbo stepped on to US soil in 1925 and had American audiences drooling from her first appearance in the silent movie *The Torrent*. She was a superstar within two years. But the coming of sound movies was a worrying time for Garbo. Would US audiences accept her foreign accent?

She made her first 'talkie' in 1930. Garbo's first lines in *Anna Christie* were: 'Gimme a vwisky vwith chincher ale on the side; and don't be stinchy, beby.' She became nicknamed the Swedish Sphinx, surrounding herself with mystery. She also earned a fortune.

Garbo never married, but had numerous love affairs. One of her lovers, Polish poet Antoni Gronowicz, told of her strange bedroom antics. He was just

Above: *A young Liz Taylor pictured by renowned photographer Baron in 1954.*

The first hit record, 'I Want You Back', came in 1970. Two years later he went solo - and those golden eggs kept on coming. His *Thriller* album published in 1982 sold 37 million copies. When its sales had reached 25 million it was estimated to have earned him $50 million. On a worldwide tour in 1988 he was earning £200 - a second!

No wonder he can afford to indulge himself with a weird lifestyle. Chimpanzee Bubbles has been trained to smile, roller-skate and ride a horse.

Jackson may be freaky himself - but he has an interest in other freaks too! While in London he showed a morbid fascination for the Victorian sideshow freak known as the Elephant Man. He visited the London Hospital in Whitechapel and stared for half an hour at the tragic remains of John Merrick, whose story was told in the film starring John Hurt.

When he returned to the US he ordered his staff to buy the preserved remains - whatever the cost. The London Hospital politely declined to sell. So Jackson bought two ancient Egyptian mummies instead.

Jackson has created a fantasy world with pet animals as a shield against his greedy human entourage

---

Howard, former president of the Jackson companies, 'Watch him next time you see him dance - you'll see the movements of Michael's menagerie right there on stage.' Added Jerome, 'Jackson lives in his own little world with his animals. He confides in them, not people. He's created a fantasy world to protect himself from the money-hungry, cut-throat humans around him who do anything they want to keep their goose laying those golden eggs.'

Michael Joe Jackson was born on 29 August, 1958 in Gary, Indiana. And he's been laying those golden eggs from the very beginning. His domineering dad, Joe, decided that his family were going to be stars, and everything was sacrificed to his dream.

His first career break came when he won a talent contest at high school. Michael's recording debut came singing with his brothers as the Jackson Five on a record called 'I'm a Big Boy Now' in 1968.

It is hardly surprising that many friends say that the key to understanding the eccentric superstar is in his troubled relationship with his father. But the singer was to get his revenge years later when he sacked his father as his manager.

He has spent his life looking for love. Michael is devoted to singer Diana Ross, who is credited with discovering the Jackson clan. Liz Taylor was next on his list. He turned one room at his mansion into a shrine to her, covering the wall with her photographs and installing a giant video screen to play her movies twenty-four hours a day. In 1987 he stunned her by proposing marriage. Liz rejected him.

Soon after this, he made enquiries about adopting four children. But it came to nothing. Then he instructed lawyers to find a surrogate mother to have his child - without sex. According to his aides, the mother would have to be one in a million - black, spiritually and physically beautiful, and with a high IQ.

Perhaps only when his child is born will Michael Jackson find true happiness and give up the bizarre childlike existence in which he so shyly hides.

ECCENTRIC FLAIR
Cranks and Crackpots

Paranoid about germs, Howard Hughes lived in a hermetically sealed environment - yet managed to run a business empire. Frank Buckland fed his pet monkeys beer in the week and port on Sundays. Cranky these two may have been, but they were not unique...

Left: *Howard Hughes and his TWA boss Joseph Bartles set off on a record-breaking Los Angeles to New York flight. Naturally the plane was filled with starlets.*

Opposite: *Film magnate, aircraft manufacturer and aviator Howard Hughes as he liked to be photographed - in the days when he allowed himself to be photographed at all.*

Below: *Starlets like the young Ginger Rogers were escorted by Howard Hughes who, with oil riches, took Hollywood by storm.*

Eccentrics have brightened every age. And now that conformity is the order of the day, with faceless bureaucrats watching and commanding our every move, they bring fresh air to our regimented lives.

HOWARD HUGHES

The twentieth-century crank Howard Hughes was one of the greatest mysteries of the modern world. He was so obsessed by germs that he cut himself off from the outside world for twenty years.

A billionaire, he lived in luxury hotels where he would always book the whole penthouse floor. He was surrounded by guards who were never allowed to see him. TV cameras monitored every possible entrance.

And inside he sealed himself off in his own prison with the most extraordinary thoroughness. All furniture was removed except for his bed and a chair. The windows were covered, so no light entered his room, and then the windows were taped to keep out germs. He had no books or photographs: just a film projector and a vast box of tissues to dust down surfaces constantly. And yet he ran a worldwide business empire with a rod of iron.

Hughes was born rich in Houston,

Above: *Visitors to the home of naturalist Frank Buckland would find alligator, mice, squirrel and ostrich on the menu.*

Texas. When his father died he left the young man an oil-drilling tool company. And twenty-one-year-old Hughes took off for Hollywood to invest in the new boom industry of movie-making.

He was an instant success, producing *Scarface*, with George Raft, and *Hell's Angels*, the first film to star Jean Harlow. She became one of his many Hollywood lovers. Hughes was charming, witty, irresistible and seriously rich. He bought apartments for his lovers as easily as some men would buy them dinners.

It was good news for a starlet to be seen with him, and he was spotted out with young hopefuls like Ava Gardner, Ginger Rogers, Mitzi Gaynor and Elizabeth Taylor.

But if he treated Hollywood and showbiz as his hobby, big business was his life. A keen pilot, he owned two aircraft companies: Trans World Airlines and Hughes Aircraft. He also saw himself as an engineer.

He designed a monster plane called Hercules to move troops in World War II. It was an eight-engined flying boat which could carry seven hundred soldiers and weighed 200 tons. But it was just too

heavy. Hughes himself was its pilot for the one mile it ever flew.

But he was already showing signs of eccentric behaviour. A police officer in Louisiana refused to believe that the scruffy tramp in front of his desk was Howard Hughes. The man was unshaven, wearing a crumpled, filthy suit, and on his feet were a scruffy pair of gym shoes.

The Louisiana police couldn't believe that the scruffy tramp in front of them was the famous billionaire businessman

---

Hughes had been taken to his police station as a vagrant. He'd crashed his private plane and, despite having $1200 in his pocket, had no identification. The police officer refused to release him until he was identified by a friend.

After his second marriage ended with a $1 million pay-off Hughes became more and more reclusive. He hired a loyal group of bodyguards who were all Mormons. They became known as the Mormon Mafia as they protected him at his bungalow in the desert near Las Vegas. Visitors were rare. But for those he dealt with, it was highly unusual. One big airline boss was driven miles into the searing heat of the desert, the car windows firmly closed. Even the air vents were sealed by paper handkerchiefs - so that their conversations could not be overheard!

For the last twenty years of his life he wandered from one luxury hotel to another with his Mormon Mafia always in attendance. To move him they often used private ambulances, with Hughes strapped to a stretcher as he left or entered his new 'home'.

His eating habits were getting stranger. Hughes was reducing himself to a skeleton. He would have an obsession about chicken soup, for instance, and that was all he would eat for weeks. Then he would go on an ice cream diet.

He only had his hair and fingernails cut twice in ten years - his nails grew to a horrendous four inches long, and his greasy hair and beard hung down his chest in a vile dirty black mass. Yet he insisted that the hairdresser clean up like a surgeon before approaching him.

He died, aged sixty-eight, on the plane which was taking him back to his birthplace in Houston, Texas. It was the one secret that he couldn't keep from the world.

FRANK BUCKLAND

Howard Hughes may have had bizarre eating habits but they were nothing compared to those of nineteenth-century naturalist Frank Buckland. He would eat anything at all - from elephant trunk to roast giraffe.

Strange eating habits ran in the family. His father, Dr William Buckland, was said to have eaten a chunk of Louis XIV's embalmed heart! Buckland senior, a clergyman and Dean of Westminster, thought the worst thing he'd ever tasted was mole - it ran a close second to stewed bluebottles.

Animals were always part of his life. He was born in 1826 and lived in a large house on the quadrangle of Christ Church, Oxford, where his father was then canon. It was full of live - and many dead - animals. Snakes and frogs were kept in glass cases in the dining room where the most extraordinary meals were served up. Alligator, mice on toast and roast ostrich were often on the menu.

Though fond of mice in batter, he could not abide fried earwigs

---

At the age of four Frank was given a small natural history cabinet which he used to store his dissections and stuffed animals. Later, while at public school, at Winchester College, he would be so hungry that he would often eat squirrel pie or mice in batter.

He kept live animals too. In his room he had a buzzard, an owl, a raccoon, jackdaws and a magpie. While he was at Oxford his pockets were stuffed with slow worms living in moss. They had a disconcerting habit of poking their heads out when he was talking.

Below: Watching, not eating... Buckland examines caged monkeys at his home. He introduced new breeds of animal to Britain; some wandered free, others he cooked.

Left: *Shropshire squire John Mytton went out hunting stark naked - even in winter - and drank up to eight bottles of port or brandy a day.*

Below: *Sir Francis Galton's* **Art of Travel** *was full of helpful hints. If you want to light your pipe while travelling in a high wind, just get your horse to lie down and use the creature as a windshield.*

Buckland became a popular surgeon at St George's Hospital, London but began to spend more and more time as a naturalist, writing and lecturing on animals. He became a founder member of the Society for the Acclimatization of Animals in the United Kingdom.

At home the living room was like a private zoo. The eccentric naturalist kept monkeys by the fire and allowed them to roam free, causing immense damage. He gave them beer every night and they had a glass of port on Sundays. Pet rats romped on his desk and a mongoose ran wild round the house.

Amidst this chaos he would work on his learned treatises, puffing away at a huge cigar and wearing a bowler hat - but with bare feet. He hated shoes and boots.

London Zoo gave him plenty of samples for his cranky menus. He insisted that a dead prize panther was dug up so that he could try panther steaks. And he was delighted when the giraffe house burnt down, because then he could try roast giraffe.

In the 1860s an interest in fish took over his life. Buckland hatched thirty thousand salmon in his kitchen and became the Inspector of HM Salmon Fisheries on the personal recommendation of Queen Victoria. He travelled around Britain by train, but he always had the carriage to himself because he smelt so appallingly of fish.

FRANCIS GALTON

Cranky scientist Francis Galton worked so hard that he was worried he would suffer from 'strained brain'. So he invented a strange hat ventilated with holes so that the cool air could circulate around his head as he studied. It had little retractable shutters which were opened by a valve, operated by a small bulb in the end of a rubber tube which hung down from the top of his head.

It seemed to work for the eccentric scientist. He was an expert in medicine, mathematics and metereology, to name just a few of his interests. He wrote prolifically, and received many academic honours as well as a knighthood.

But the dotty scientist will always be remembered for one serious discovery. He was the man who realized that every human being has a different set of fingerprints, a revelation that was to change the face of police detective work. His system of classifying them is still used today.

One of his most successful works was a book called *The Art of Travel*. Published in the 1840s, it suggested a cure for feeling under the weather while travelling in foreign countries: drop a little gunpowder into a glass of warm soapy water, and drink. It will tickle the throat, he said, but clear the system.

He had many such helpful suggestions. How do you keep your clothes dry in a downpour? Take them off and sit on them. Blisters on the feet? Make a lather of soap bubbles in your socks and break a raw egg into each boot.

How do you light your pipe in a heavy wind? Get your horse to lie down and use it as a windshield. To cure wasp stings: take the gunge from your pipe and smear it on the skin.

Galton was born in 1822 into a rich scientifically minded family. After Cambridge University he travelled in Syria, Egypt and the Sudan. He acted the typical Englishman abroad, while at the same time taking his scientific research seriously.

There were no carpets, curtains or wallpaper in Galton's home because he regarded them as purposeless dust-traps

---

He wanted to know why the Hottentot women had such large bottoms. Seeing a suitable example bathing one day he set to work to do some serious research. At a distance he measured her rear with his sextant and then using trigonometry and logarithms, calculated her shape in comparison with the standard English woman. It made a very solemn paper for the Royal Geographical Society.

At his London home in South Kensington, he insisted that everything should have a practical purpose. He refused to have carpets, curtains and wallpaper - because they collected dust and had no purpose. He had no comfortable chairs, just wooden benches.

Diners at his Rutland Gate home were also unwitting victims of his experiments. He had a theory that if people were attracted to each other they would lean towards each other like metal to a magnet. If they weren't attracted they would sit bolt upright. He installed pressure pads on the sides of his dining room chairs, and after his guests had left took readings to judge if they had got on.

JOHN MYTTON

Shropshire squire, John Mytton drank up to eight bottles of port or brandy every day. He used to say that it kept him warm while he was out hunting stark naked ... whatever the weather.

Mytton was born in 1796, and when his father died he was left the family seat, Halston Hall, near Shrewsbury, £60,000 in cash and an income of about £10,000 a year. It was a fortune in those days, but he got through the lot in fifteen years.

He dropped bundles of notes around his estate. He gave money to his servants without asking them to account for it. After winning thousands of pounds at Doncaster races he lost it all when it blew away as he tried to count it.

Squire Mytton rode a light carriage around as if he was a Roman charioteer. He purposely drove into a rabbit hole to see if it would turn over. It did.

To the local people he was a hero, to the county set he was an idiot. But he didn't care what they thought. He would shock his friends by arriving at posh dinner parties in full hunting gear and riding a brown bear. On one occasion he was spurring on his steed so hard that the bear turned round and bit him.

But in 1830 Mytton ran out of money. Sodden with drink, with the creditors closing in on him, he escaped to France. There he had one last escapade that is remembered. Getting hiccups one night, he recalled that a sudden shock would cure them. So he set fire to his nightshirt. The hiccups vanished instantly but he was badly burned.

After returning to England he was sent to a debtors' prison. He died in 1838, aged only thirty-eight.

TWINS
Double Identity

Twins - identical, non-identical and Siamese - must be the ultimate examples of shared lives. Telepathic communication, fear of the outside world, and sinister control of each other often figure in their strange existences

The number of twins born every year is growing - and no one knows why! A study in Britain revealed that 7452 pairs arrived in 1990. That works out at about one set in every ninety pregnancies. Now doctors are trying to discover exactly what is causing the upsurge in these bumper bundles.

Twins are created by the fertilization of two separate eggs by two separate sperm, and develop in two separate placentas. They may be no more alike than any other brothers and sisters.

Such twins may run in families, usually on the mother's side. More fascinating are identical twins, caused when a single egg, fertilized by a single sperm, divides into two. The babies share the same placenta and are always the same sex. The chances of having twins increases over the age of thirty-five. And the likelihood of twins increases with the more babies a mother has.

That is the medical explanation and definition of twins. But to mothers throughout history - and nowdays to an increasing number of them - having two-in-one-go means double trouble and amazing stories that are worth a second look.

Opposite: *Identical twins are caused when a single egg fertilized by a single sperm divides into two.*

Below: *Greta and Freda Chaplin eat, work and sleep in unison. If separated they cry. By their teens they had synchronized every single movement.*

BRITAIN'S ODDEST COUPLE?

Perhaps the most famous twins of the 1990s are Greta and Freda Chaplin. They speak and eat in unison, do literally everything together and cry if they are separated for even a moment.

When they dress they face each other as if looking in a mirror. If Freda wears a bracelet on her left wrist, then Greta will wear one on her right. If one breaks a shoelace, the other immediately pulls the lace from her opposite shoe. They buy the same-size shoes, even though Greta's feet are larger than her twin sister's. If Freda grazes her right arm and needs a plaster, Greta will put one on the same spot on her left arm.

Every movement, down to fastening the last button, is carried out in absolute unison. When they sweep the floor they both hold the vacuum cleaner. When they make tea they both carry the pot to the table. If they are given clothes that are slightly different they alter them to make them match.

For instance, if one twin is given black gloves and the other green gloves, they will

Right: Film-maker Emeric Pressburger wanted identical twin girls for his movie Twice Upon a Time. *These two were at the audition.*

Below: A children's party was one of the test scenes for Twice Upon a Time. *Here some 200 twins watch a conjuring show to make them less self-conscious.*

swap one. They even exchange the buttons on their coats so that they appear identical.

When they eat they insist on having exactly the same-size portions on their plate. If they're having fish and chips they will both pick up a chip at exactly the same time.

When they walk, their footsteps are in precise rhythm. They brush their teeth at exactly the same time and pace. Their hair is pinned up in exactly the same way and their clothes are identical down to stockings, handkerchiefs and underwear.

A social worker once gave the twins two different-coloured bars of soap, and they burst into tears. Both bars had to be

cut in half and divided between them before they would use it.

And the twins get through a lot of soap. One of their obsessive rituals is bathing. They like to spend up to two hours a day washing each other, and get through fourteen bars of soap a week.

If one woman falls ill, so does the other.

The Chaplins are obsessive about their bathing ritual and get through fourteen bars of soap a week

---

The Chaplins say they can remember nothing about their schooldays - they went to their local Derwent Junior School and Birnholme Secondary School in York - or indeed their growing years. But it is believed that the sisters, who were forty-eight when their lifestyles were first fully studied in 1991, developed their strange obsessions because of the strictness of their mother.

From the time they were babies their mother treated them as one and encouraged their total dependence on each other, virtually to the exclusion of the rest of the world. The toys they played with as little girls were identical - right down to their twin dolls. Ask the women what advice their mother gave them, and they reply in unison: 'She told us to always stick to each other and never to go with men.'

The sisters were even told that if they went to the shops they had to buy two of everything. If only one purchase was available, they had to go without.

If one sister wanted to read and the other didn't, neither was allowed to read. Even their individual names were dropped and both were simply called 'Twin'. They were discouraged from finding outside friends.

It was hardly surprising then that by the time the girls were fifteen their every movement was totally synchronized. And although their bizarre pattern of behaviour was caused by their obsessive mother Elsie, it had now become too much for her to cope with.

After much deliberation, she and her retired bus driver husband Jack decided that the girls should be put into care. The Chaplin girls were then to spend more

than a decade cooped up in various hostels - a strange existence for a strange couple.

Sadly though, right up until their parents died in 1989, the twins would make the journey every week to their old home on the Tang Estate in York. After getting off the bus, they would walk to the semi-detached house and simply stand and look. They had long given up ringing the doorbell. It was never answered.

They could see their mother in the house fully aware her estranged daughters were outside but refusing to accept their presence. She acted as if she couldn't see them.

But still the sisters visited. They just looked, sometimes standing motionless for hours before finally both turning away at the same moment and going home.

At fifteen the twins were rejected by the mother who had brought them up in such a bizarre fashion, and were put into care

---

The Chaplin twins now live quietly in London and do not like attention or being surrounded by people, despite the fact that their very lifestyle and appearance draw attention to them. Shopping is an ordeal, as they feel that everyone is staring at them. Sometimes they will go out of their front door and head straight back inside again because they both instinctively feel that something is not right. They do not need to speak a word.

Above: *Allie and Marnie Anderson were the twin teen daughters of a London film producer. Many such twins find life unsettling.*

Above: *Being a mother of identical twin babies can be doubly joyful - or just double trouble.*

Together, they say: 'We don't like being stared at. Sometimes we shout: "Go away! What are you looking at?"'

They have had other obsessions, too. They hit the headlines when they latched on to a next-door neighbour, Kevin Iveson. They followed the unfortunate man everywhere, pestered him at his working men's club and even threw themselves in front of his van.

Despite doing all he could to deal patiently with the odd couple who followed him everywhere, sixty-six-year-old war hero Mr Iveson finally snapped. After all, he had put up with their continual presence for a staggering fifteen years.

During that time the women had trapped his hand in a door and written him a series of poison pen letters. On one occasion when they hurled abuse at him, Mr Iveson turned on his tape recorder. He reckoned no one could possibly believe what he had to endure. That recording was used in evidence when the twins

were taken to court in November 1980.

But despite the foolproof evidence, the twins repeatedly denied the allegations, stunning the court with their constant interruptions (in unison of course) of: 'He is a liar. We have never been near him.'

A consultant psychiatrist said there was no medical explanation or solution to their problem. The Chaplin women were convicted of causing a breach of the peace. They were released from prison early when they promised to stop pestering Mr Iveson. They were also terrified that being in prison would one day mean separation.

Despite Kevin Iveson's tapes of the abuse the two women had hurled at him, in court they denied all knowledge of him

---

Their unique case created much publicity and the twins withdrew even more into their singular, secret world. They couldn't understand why people were taking an interest in them and it scared them. They ignored the strangers who wrote to them. All except for one man who was to provide the women with a more normal lifestyle and help to bring them back into the real world.

They had no reason to trust retired engineer Jack Davenport, but something inside them told them they should. And Jack felt genuinely sorry for the women.

He offered them accommodation in his London house. 'I felt I could help them,' he said. 'They seemed starved of kindness, affection and understanding. I was ready to offer all those things.'

Greta and Freda arrived for what was initially to be a trial visit. But Jack proved to be their saviour and the three became good friends. For the first time in their lives the women learned how to open tins of food, how to cook properly and how to look after themselves. Jack became their protector and father figure.

And he gave them the confidence eventually to move out to a place of their own, although they still visit him daily.

The women still cannot be separated. If that happens, even for a moment, they become hysterical and run around in circles. They don't like crowds, and are still unable to contend with abuse and stares.

An even greater criminal dilemma was the case of baby-faced identical twins Craig and Timmy Good. They were just fifteen years of age when their father William and grandmother Cleo were shot dead in their trailer home on Saluda Island, South Carolina. Hauled before a court accused of the murders, the twins blamed each other for pulling the trigger of the .22 rifle.

The boys had been double trouble ever since their birth in 1973. They seemed to have a psychic knowledge of whatever the other was thinking or doing. At school they would swap classrooms to confuse their teachers.

By the time they were nine they were already selling drugs for their father, William. On the few occasions when they managed to attend school they were often suspended for smoking marijuana, fighting, drunkenness or setting off the fire alarms.

William Good, long separated from his wife Robbie, bought the boys rifles for Christmas just before he was killed.

William and his sixty-year-old mother Cleo were murdered on 20 February 1989. Her rings were wrenched from her fingers and her chequebook and pick-up truck stolen. Police believed a psychotic killer was on the loose and began a search for what they assumed would be the butchered bodies of the twins. In fact they found them stoned on drugs, living in the laundry room of an apartment block. A social worker said he believed the boys had killed their father and grandmother 'so they could party with their drug-smoking, school-cutting, beer-drinking friends'.

Police assumed a psychotic killer was responsible for the murders and expected to find the twins dead too

---

The twins were tried as adults. Timmy testified that his brother fired the fatal shot. Craig, however, refused to take the stand but in a statement said he saw his father and grandmother 'fall' - though he did not see Timmy pull the trigger.

Below: *Identical twins can share a form of telepathic communication. Even when they are far apart they often seem to be aware of the other's feelings.*

The prosecutor, district attorney Don Myers, told the jury that it did not matter which twin actually pulled the trigger - both were equally guilty. He said: 'It was sickening to have to sit and listen to these twins talk casually about the murders as if they were nothing. They have no remorse. They think it's a big joke and their only regret is getting caught.'

The jury took four hours to decide whether or not only one twin had undertaken the killings while the other took no part. In the end they agreed with district attorney Myers and found them both guilty of murder. They were each sentenced to life imprisonment for the killings, and sixty-five years each for armed robbery and stealing an automobile.

When Eric Bocock and Tommy Marriott met for the first time in thirty-eight years, they looked at each other in amazement. Separated at birth, the identical twins greeted one another wearing the same hairstyle, the same neatly trimmed beard and gold-rimmed glasses.

Both were dressed in velvet jackets, white shirts, grey trousers and black shoes. Both were 5ft 6in tall and both weighed exactly 12st 6lb.

It was even more bizarre for them to discover that they had both been chargehands at engineering works for twenty-one years. Both had their hair cut by their wives, both had an allergy to house dust and both liked horse racing.

Their astonishing meeting was recorded for television in 1983 when a TV company helped Eric trace his long-lost brother. Professor Thomas Bouchard of the University of Minnesota, where doctors were carrying out a study of identical twins, said it was the most striking case of 'twinned lives' he had ever witnessed.

FOR EVER JOINED

But the most fascinating twins of all are those known as 'Siamese' - or in scientific jargon, pygopagous. Britain's first and most celebrated Siamese twins (although at that time they were not known as such) were 'Ye Maydes of Biddenden' in Kent.

Born around 1100, they were joined together at both the hips and the shoulders. The girls, Eliza and Mary Chulkhurst, lived for thirty-four years and expired within six hours of each other - the longest-surviving twin supposedly declaring: 'As we came together we shall also go together.'

To this day they are remembered by locals in the village, who bake Biddenden Maid cakes every Easter Monday.

The Biddenden Maids never married or even fell in love, as far as legend has it. But Siamese twins can and do form romantic attachments - sometimes causing trouble in double doses, sometimes not.

Rosa and Josefa Blazek were born in 1880 in Czechoslovakia. They were joined together at the pelvis, having two lungs and two hearts but only one stomach.

In 1907 the twins met a German officer. Rosa married him and had a baby boy, Franz, who was seven years of age when his father died in World War I. The sisters went on to earn a fortune by touring with circuses and peep shows throughout Europe and North America. They had very different personalities, but never allowed them to interfere with their calm and trusting relationship. For instance, Josefa drank only beer while her sister could take only wine; this caused considerable upsets in their single stomach but not once in their friendship!

When one twin got jaundice, their shared stomach enabled the other to eat for two

In 1922 Josefa contracted jaundice while appearing in Chicago. Rosa ate for two in order to keep up her sister's strength but she refused to allow surgeons to separate them to save her life. She said: 'If Josefa dies, I want to die too.' She did...only fifteen minutes after her twin.

The most famous twins of all time were Chang and Eng, the Siamese twins born to Chinese parents on 11 May 1811, in the province of Mekong, Siam. Joined firmly at the chest by a six-inch-long band of flesh, the children were

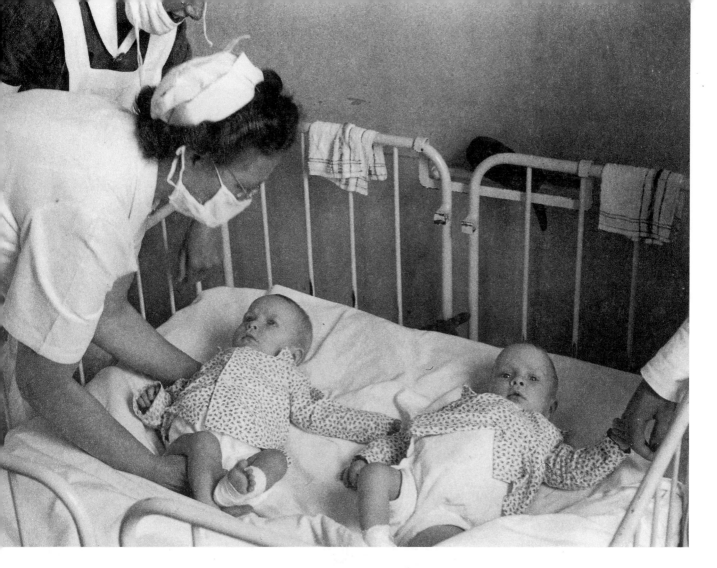

sentenced to die by the King of Siam who believed them to be an omen of ill fortune for his country.

Instead, a Scottish merchant named Robert Hunter took them to America where they grew up to become two utterly different personalities.

Chang was an extrovert with an early thirst for life and a later thirst for bourbon whiskey. Eng, on the other hand, was a feeble child who had a struggle to survive and who later abhorred his brother's wild ways. He was, as one might expect, strictly teetotal. Chang once faced a prison sentence for a drunken assault but was let off because the judge thought it unfair on Eng.

The twins became a sideshow attraction, touring the world. In France they caused a furore because it was believed their appearance could cause deformation of unborn children. In England, which they visited in 1829, they were feted by the nobility and gawped at by the common crowds. Eventually, tiring of their lives on the road, they settled down as farmers in North Carolina,

assuming the surname Bunker.

At the age of 44 they married two expatriate English sisters, Sarah Ann, aged twenty-six, and Adelaide Yates, twenty-eight. They all shared a very large bed and the sisters gave birth to no fewer than twenty-one children, all of them perfectly healthy. To show that there was no impropriety in the relationship with their wives, they purchased two houses - one for Sarah Ann and one for Adelaide - and they stayed with the sisters on alternate weeks.

A newspaper report of the time states: 'A most pathetic characteristic of these illustrious brothers was the affection and forbearance they showed for each other until shortly before their death.

'They bore each other's trials and petty maladies with the greatest sympathy, and in this manner rendered their lives far more agreeable than a casual observer would suppose possible.'

Their death, when it came on 17 January 1874, was peaceful. It is believed that they both died of old age at exactly the same moment.

Above: *Three-week-old Siamese twins Folkje and Tjitske de Vries start life apart in hospital in Holland after they were separated to begin a normal life in 1954.*

SALVADOR DALI
Surrealist Prankster

The most outrageous showman of the twentieth-century art world, Salvador Dali turned his whole life into an expression of Surrealism - presenting the grotesquely improbable as a normal everyday event.

Salvador Dali, the great Surrealist painter, was as eccentric and splashy as his fantastic and memorable dreamscapes. In fact, when he died in January 1989 at the ripe old age of eighty-four, he left behind a legacy of bizarre behaviour to match his enigmatic works - a fitting epitaph for one of the leading artistic showmen of this century.

Unlike many of his peers, the Spanish-born genius was a perennial attention-seeker, and was often pilloried as a madman who was far more interested in cold hard cash than in art. The 'Divine Dali', as he liked to call himself, was an unforgettable character with his long, slicked-down hair and waxed moustache, and a true international oddball, flitting between New York, Paris and a castle in Spain, sporting an ermine cape and a silver-handled cane.

'Every morning upon awakening, I experience a supreme pleasure: that of being Salvador Dali'

But in a career that spanned almost six decades he produced approximately two thousand serious artistic works, wrote and illustrated books, poems and essays, did stage designs for plays and ballets, produced commercial advertisements, wrote an autobiography and designed

Opposite: *Renegade surrealist artist Salvador Dali relaxes characteristically in a six-legged chair at his home near Cadaques on the Spanish Coast.*

Below left: *Dali with his Russian-born wife and constant source of inspiration, Gala Dimitrovna Diaharoff.*

Below: *He used skulls, bones and entrails in his paintings. Here he wears one of his props while clowning at his Mediterranean beach home.*

everything from jewellery and furniture to glass and china.

THE ECCENTRIC EGOTIST

Beyond his undeniable talent, Dali was wonderfully, almost uniquely, weird and egotistical, repeatedly claiming he was the greatest artist of modern times. 'Every morning upon awakening, I experience a supreme pleasure: that of being Salvador Dali, and I ask myself, wonder-struck, what prodigious thing will he do today,' he once said.

On his first visit to America in the early 1930s - with money borrowed from his colleague Pablo Picasso - Dali unveiled for reporters who met him at the ship a nude painting of his companion, Gala Dimitrovna Diaharoff, with lamb chops on her shoulder. Asked about the chops, he replied: 'Very simple. I love [her] and I love lamb chops. Here they are together. Perfect harmony.'

Just days later, while giving a lecture in New York, he appeared in a deep-sea diving suit and helmet. 'The better', he explained with grave seriousness, 'to descend into the depths of the subconscious.' Unfortunately, he almost suffocated because he'd forgotten to bring along an air pump.

In 1974 Dali, who seemed willing to do just about anything if the price was

Above: *His paradise villa at Port Lligat where he 'descended into the depths of subconsciousness'.*

Below: *He called himself the Divine Dali. His detractors called him a cash-orientated showman. His admirers saw him as a genius. The world found him unforgettable.*

right, signed on with a US advertising agency for a television commercial in which he painted a leotard-clad model to illustrate how Alka-Seltzer works.

Later, after leaving New York for France, he was seen carrying a 5 ft tall, purple Bugs Bunny doll that had been given to him as a farewell present. 'This is the most ugly and frightening animal in the world,' he said. 'I will paint it with mayonnaise and make it an object of art.'

When a reporter once visited him at his home on Spain's Costa Brava, the artist waved him into the garden and suggested: 'Let's climb that tree where we can be comfortable.' Two armchairs were hanging in the branches!

Although he was married to Gala until her death in 1982, he had no children, and he had always maintained he didn't want it any other way. 'Great geniuses always produce mediocre children, and I do not want to go through that experience,' he said. 'I am only interested in inheriting myself.'

He would say anything to shock and outrage. He once exulted: 'Sometimes I spit on the portrait of my mother from sheer pleasure.'

Dali's eccentricity was a by-product of his refusal to take art as seriously as his fellow artists did. When other Surrealists

announced they were Communists, Dali come out as a fervent Spanish royalist. When other artists said the only real path to artistic prominence was through poverty and bohemian simplicity, he could not resist telling everyone he met that he was in it for the money and the luxuries it could bring. And when modern artists said that the truth could be arrived at through avant-garde experimentation, Dali announced that he was actually an old-fashioned painter.

Through it all, Dali insisted he was about the only sane person in the world, as he revealed in his 1976 autobiography, *The Unspeakable Confessions of Salvador Dali*: 'The clown is not I, but rather our monstrously cynical and so naïvely unconscious society that plays at the game of being serious, the better to hide its own madness. For I - I can never repeat it enough - am not mad.'

Dali's greatness as an artist probably reached its zenith between the mid-1920s and the early 1940s, when the Surrealist period was similarly at its peak. Many of his paintings of that era were famous for their strange placement of unrelated objects in an environment where they did not belong, such as *The Persistence of Memory* of 1931 - which many critics still regard as one of the finest examples of Surrealism – in which he draped limp watches over various objects, including a branch of a dead tree. Dali, who loved to babble, said the watches were 'nothing else than the tender, extravagant, solitary, paranoiac-critical Camembert of time and space'.

THE PRECIOUS GENIUS

Salvador Felipe Jacinto Dali was born into a middle-class family in the town of Figueras in Upper Catalonia, Spain, on 11 May 1904, two years after the death of a brother who was also named Salvador. But in his crazy way, Dali would even argue that fact. Instead, he often said that he was born two months earlier because, he was quite certain, he began to think while still a seven-month-old foetus. 'It was warm, it was soft, it was silent,' he claimed. 'It was paradise.'

From a very early age, he wished to be an artist, and by the time he was ten he

had already completed two flamboyant oil paintings, *Helen of Troy* and *Joseph Greeting His Brethren*. But he was also a rather weird youngster, and loved the attention he got from stunts like flinging himself down a long flight of stairs at school. And his favourite place at home was a big tub in the laundry room, where he would sit for hours, thinking and painting. He also liked to wear his hair long under a large black hat, and would later describe himself as the world's first hippie.

When he turned seventeen, his father sent him to the San Fernando Academy of Fine Arts in Madrid, where he not only won several prizes but also managed to get himself suspended for twelve months for allegedly inciting other students to riot over the appointment of a professor who he thought was unworthy. He returned a year later, only to be kicked out for good in 1926 for what the academy said was his support for revolutionary causes.

Although his early years were influenced by a variety of styles, in 1928, on a visit to Paris, he was introduced to

Top: *Dali claimed that he began to think while still a foetus. What he was thinking in later life was to most people much more of a mystery.*

Above: *His long, waxed moustache was the trademark of a man who courted publicity - which helped his improbable works sell for millions.*

Surrealism by his fellow Spanish artist Joan Miro. Founded in 1924 by the French poet Andre Breton, the Surrealist movement advocated the 'systematic exploration of the subconscious imagination' and Dali soon became one of the leaders of the movement.

SEXUAL IMAGERY

In 1929 he painted *The Great Masturbator*, one of his more significant paintings of the period. It depicts a large, wax-like head with pink cheeks and closed eyes with very long eyelashes. A huge nose leans on the ground, and instead of a mouth there is a rotting grasshopper

crawling with ants. For much of the 1930s, sexual and scatological images were a common theme in his work, and he had a bizarre fondness for including in them grasshoppers, telephones, ants, keys, melting torsos, crutches, bread and hair. Dali called his technique the 'handmade photography of concrete irrationality' and it was based, he said, on 'the associations and interpretations of delirious phenomena'. Not surprisingly, even he said he didn't understand all his images!

During the 1930s his fellow Surrealists grew worried about Dali's preoccupation with Hitler's genitals

---

Although his work was well received by critics who praised the deep vistas of his paintings, critical success did not bring instant profit. Instead, Dali plied the streets of Paris vainly trying to find buyers for his bizarre inventions - devices like women's shoes with high steel springs, fingernail-shaped looking glasses, and even a plaster head of a roaring lion with a fried egg in its mouth.

His eccentricity, however, led to a falling out with his fellow Surrealists, who expelled him from the movement in 1934, claiming he had developed an unhealthy interest in money and was guilty of 'vulgarisation and academicism'.

DECLINE AND DISARRAY

Over the remaining decades of his life, he spent more and more time on a variety of business and commercial affairs. For several years he did one large painting a year - usually for a huge fee - and became involved in everything from selling lithographs to designing shirts and bathing suits to making airline commercials. 'Dali sleeps best after receiving a tremendous quantity of cheques,' he used to say. He must have slept like a baby because he lent his name to perfumes, body-freezing schemes, brandy bottles and furniture and fabrics. His commercials led most critics to agree that the last two decades or so of his working life were remarkable more for their plain silliness than for any real artistic accomplishment.

Below: *Publicity seeker Dali poses with a local fisherman's son and starfish on the rocks near his home. The bay was given to the artist by Spanish dictator General Franco.*

In later life his lust for money became an obsession and he lent his name to everything from perfumes to body-freezing schemes

One of the sillier schemes was his painting in 1973 of the wall panels for a fleet of Iberia passenger planes. In the years just prior to his death Dali suffered from a variety of health problems, including Parkinson's disease, deep depression and malnutrition. After the death of Gala, he spent most of the time at his twelfth-century castle at Pubol, north of Barcelona, but in August 1984 a short circuit in a device he used to summon his nurses set fire to his bedclothes. Badly burned and too weak to stay at the castle any longer, he was moved to a wing of the Dali Museum in Figueras, where he had been born, by his assistants. Tragically, for the next five years he lingered largely in a horrid limbo, confined to a wheelchair and fed through a tube. The hands that had painted some of the most important art of the twentieth century shook uncontrollably.

His professional life was similarly in complete disarray. Secretaries and agents milked him for all he was worth, selling copyright and reproduction rights to his works all over the world - with much of the profit going into their own pockets.

*Left: **The artist slumbers. He once said, 'Dali sleeps best after receiving tremendous quantities of cheques.' He did.***

*Below: **Dali and his wife Gala. After her death he spent most of his time at his 12th century castle north of Barcelona. His final years were spent in pitiful decline.***

Dali's unfortunate habit of signing blank sheets of paper led to a flourishing trade in fakes

Fake Dali lithographs were everywhere - a process encouraged by the artist's disheartening habit in the 1970s of regularly signing blank pieces of paper. Dali could and did sign more than 1800 an hour, according to one associate.

Not surprisingly, the art world was scandalized by forgeries of his works, and Dali himself was said to have signed thousands of blank sheets of paper for easy conversion into bogus Dali 'originals'. By some estimates, the forgeries of his work ran into hundreds of millions of dollars.

Still, Dali himself was not perturbed by the furore. 'No one would worry if I were a mediocre painter,' he sniffed. 'All the great painters have been falsified.' Indeed, he remained overwhelmingly popular with art lovers, and in 1979 and 1980 a major retrospective drew more than a million visitors in Paris and 250,000 in London.

And for all his failings, Dali remains, even in death, an unforgettable character, who made eccentricity an art form. As the critic Winthrop Sargeant once remarked: 'There is nothing abnormal about Dali. He is simply antinormal!'

RASPUTIN
Peasant Turned Seer

Before the 1917 Revolution St Petersburg society was scandalized by a newcomer in its midst. How did a filthy, semi-literate peasant from Siberia, member of a sex-obsessed 'holy cult', exert a hypnotic influence over the ruling family of Imperial Russia?

Right: *Asked by Princess Murat for the secret of his powers, he wrote: 'It is love, my little dove.'*

Opposite: *An honoured equal...Rasputin the 'mad monk' seated with Captain Von Lohman of a crack cavalry regiment and Prince Pontiatine, chamberlain of the royal palaces.*

Below: *Dressed as a monk, Grigori Rasputin held an eerie power over weak-willed Tsar Nicholas II.*

R arely has an individual wielded as much power as the 'mad monk', Grigori Rasputin, over a monarch and supreme ruler. The weak-minded Nicholas II, Tsar of all the Russias, saw his wife, the Tsarina Alexandra, fall under his spell and witnessed his own influence wane as the demonic-eyed holy man exerted more and more sway over the court. In death, as in life, Rasputin defied belief. It took poison, gunshots, a beating with chains and finally drowning to polish him off.

THE SIBERIAN PEASANT BOY

Rasputin was born in the farthest of Imperial Russia's outposts: Siberia. He was christened in the Russian Orthodox Church as Grigori Novykh, only later answering to the name of 'Rasputin' which, translated, means 'debauched one', a tag he wore with evil delight.

The name 'Rasputin' means 'the debauched one', and he delighted in it

---

Siberia then, as now, was the home of exiles and banished enemies of the state. Life was brutal and harsh among the villages dotting the endless plains: particularly harsh in the village of Pokrovskoye, where Rasputin's parents tilled miserable plots of thin soil and raised a few chickens. In 1872 Anna, a Mongol girl from Tobolsk, gave birth to her third child, Grigori.

The boy was destined for a life of hard work, rustic living and probably an early death. But two things marked him out: his intense, burning eyes and an incredible, seemingly insatiable, lust for the opposite sex.

He lost his virginity to a Russian general's wife, Danilova Kubasova, who, with the aid of six handmaidens, seduced him in her bedchamber in their stately home near his village.

After that his sexual exploits among the local populace were legendary. He frequently promenaded with prostitutes in his native village, and earned the scorn of all when he was caught frolicking in a pond with three girls: even though then, at the age of twenty, he had already married a local girl, Praskovia Feodorovna.

Rasputin claimed that his religious transformation took place while bathing naked in a pond with some village girls

---

It was during his cold-water dip with the village maidens, Rasputin would later claim, that a religious transformation overcame him. This sudden enlightenment caused him to uproot and take to the primitive roads and farm tracks of Russia, leaving behind his three children, to preach the heretical and somewhat confused gospel of the strange religious sect of a group known as the Khlisti. Rasputin entered a Khlisti monastery at Verkhoture where his debauchery was honed.

Bizarre sexual customs, multi-partner relationships and orgies were all part of their gospel: they believed that in order to be redeemed, man must first sin. It was a perfect cult for the over-sexed Rasputin.

Thus converted, Rasputin began the wanderings that would eventually lead to the court of the Tsar. Russia was then a primitive, pre-industrial land, and news of Rasputin's deeds was spread largely by word of mouth. He took on the eminence of a holy man, becoming imbued with undeserved mysticism as he doled out snake-oil cures to the peasantry and preached the gospel of indulgence.

He began preaching about 'redemption

through sexual release' and told the poor people whom he encountered that it was their duty before God to surrender to him their wives, daughters and any other female relations.

ARRIVING IN ST PETERSBURG

Soon he landed up in St Petersburg, the glorious Western-style capital of Imperial Russia. For Rasputin, St Petersburg was the natural place to be. He set himself up in an apartment on a fashionable street and invited ladies - his reputation by then, 1903, was considerable - to dine at his table before inviting them to what he dubbed his 'holy of holies', the bedchamber!

Upper class women discovered a new and thrilling sensation in making love with this filthy, drunken 'holy man'

Typically, day after day Rasputin could be found in his house, surrounded by beautiful young women: he called them his 'disciples'. More often than not he sat with one on his lap, lecturing about the 'mysterious resurrection' that awaited all his conquests.

To understand his entry into the very highest circles of Russian political and social life it is necessary to understand the mind of the monarch himself. Tsar Nicholas was a charming, autocratic, sensitive but weak leader, out of step with the great social and political changes sweeping the world. He had been brought up to revere the divine right of kings, to believe that he was God's missionary on earth to look after the great mass of peoples that made up Holy Russia. He was sadly deluded.

His rule started in 1894 with a pronouncement that he would reign as his forebears had: as a total autocrat. He paid no heed to the growing dissatisfaction within his country, the great revolutionary movement that was growing daily, even though his secret police force, the Okhrana, warned him of the danger of Marxism and Leninism.

Two years after Rasputin's arrival in St Petersburg, revolution occurred in Russia. Workers, hungry for bread, marched peacefully on the grand Winter

Below: *Two things marked Rasputin out, right from the start - extraordinarily piercing eyes, and an unshakable lust for women.*

Palace. Dozens were cut down by gunfire outside the gates by loyal Cossacks and police; the snow turned red with their blood as they tried to present to their ruler a petition demanding change.

Unmoved by the dead the Tsar said afterwards: 'Under no circumstances will I ever agree to a representative form of government, for I consider it harmful to the trust of God.'

Tsar Nicholas believed he had been invested with a divine right to rule his people, and rejected all other forms of government

---

Tsar Nicholas was striving to preserve an old order that guaranteed poverty and misery for the masses and splendour and indulgence for the aristocracy. It was the latter which attracted Rasputin, who had garnered a reputation for himself as a holy man with healing powers.

Tales were told of biblical-style 'laying on of hands' performed by Rasputin in the villages and towns he passed through. Whether or not he actually had any attributes other than an over-sized sexual appetite is not known. But at the time he seemed a blessing to the Tsarina Alexandra as she worried for the health of the young Tsarevitch, the Crown Prince Alexis: for the boy was a haemophiliac.

Above: *The mad monk surrounded by his fawning court followers. The faithful were granted a 'laying on of hands' by the mystical Rasputin.*

Below: *A drawing of Rasputin by the Princess Lucien Murat. The monk preached a philosophy of self-indulgent sex worship.*

Alexandra was strong-willed and the true power behind the Romanov throne. Summoned by the Tsarina to test his powers of healing, in 1908 Rasputin made his first visit to the Winter Palace to see the ailing Tsarevitch.

When Rasputin first appeared at the Winter Palace it was during one of the boy's bleeding fits. He paid no heed to protocol in his visit and arrived unkempt from a bedroom session with the wife of a general. By some means, probably crude hypnotism, those who witnessed him calm the young lad testified that he did indeed possess strange and mystical powers. The boy's internal agony ceased, and the bleeding stopped.

The mad monk arrived at the Winter Palace dirty and dishevelled, straight from the bed of a general's wife

---

For the Tsarina his arrival and miracle working were a blessing she would never forget. From that day forward the fortunes of Holy Russia, the Romanov dynasty and the unholy fakir were inextricably bound together.

Conservative ministers and nobles, outraged by his behaviour with some of the highest women in the land, pleaded with the Tsar to banish him: but at first to no avail. Finally, he was forced to see reason when his chief minister Stolypin sent him a dossier of Rasputin's sexual misdeeds. This time the Tsar had no choice but to exile Rasputin.

But his departure in 1911 signalled a turn for the worse in the health of young Alexander. Within six months the Tsarina had gained his release from internal exile and he was once again admitted to the grand salons of the Winter Palace. He reached the pinnacle of his power four years later as Russia was bleeding itself to death on the battlefield against the Tsar's cousin Kaiser Wilhelm. The situation was so dire that the Tsar left St Petersburg for the front to assume command. Alexandra was left behind to assume supreme power. But although she was the acting head of state, it was Rasputin who became the real ruler of Russia. His influence ranged from the appointment of Church officials to the selection of cabinet ministers.

THE MADMAN WHO WOULD NOT DIE

His conduct outraged the nobles, who saw him as an affront to civilized behaviour: but they were powerless while he held the Tsarina in his sway. In 1916 Prince Feliks Yusupov, husband of the Tsar's niece, formed a conspiracy to end the mad monk's life.

Together with Vladimir Mitrofanovich Puriskevich and Grand Duke Dimitry Pavlovich, the Tsar's cousin, Yusupov decided to invite Rasputin to his home for supper: a final poisoned repast that would snuff the life from him. Rasputin accepted readily.

In the basement of the Moika Palace, at midnight on 29 December, Rasputin tucked heartily into food sprinkled with cyanide. While 'Yankee Doodle Dandee' played on a phonograph in the room above, Rasputin asked for more. Then he began to look drunk, his eyes swimming, and he asked the prince to sing for him!

Yusupov ran to his friends in the room above to tell them Rasputin had not died, and went back with a loaded revolver. The prince then fired two shots into him and he went down. 'But he was not dead,' said Yusupov. 'He was gasping and roaring like a wounded animal and grabbed me by the throat.'

Above: *Ragged-bearded Rasputin was found guilty of a catalogue of sexual indiscretions with the wives of noblemen. He was banished to the hinterland in 1911.*

He staggered through the doorway into the freezing courtyard where the victim showed remarkable stamina by surviving four more bullets. He was still alive when the prince and other conspirators finally silenced him by beating him with chains. He was then weighted down and dragged to the Neva River.

With his death the conspirators hoped that the Tsar would disentangle the political and social mess created by his wife under Rasputin. It had gone too deep into Russian society; within months the entire Romanov dynasty was dead.

History's epitaph for Rasputin was best summed up by the moderate revolutionary Alexander Kerensky, who said: 'If there had been no Rasputin, there would have been no Lenin.'